WHEN YOU CAN'T REMEMBER SHIITAKE

WHEN YOU CAN'T REMEMBER SHIITAKE

Debbie Klein
Illustrated by Dalton McGuire

ISBN: 1983466050
ISBN-13: 9781983466052
Library of Congress Control Number: 2018900368
CreateSpace Independent Publishing Platform
North Charleston, South Carolina

Dedicated to my sister, Babs

Part One

Welcome to My World

Getting older is a part of life, and if you play your cards right, it can be the best part, too! Wisdom and humor are the magnificent gifts of old age. We've been there, done that, and we know how your story ends before you finish telling it.

The expectations of youth are exhausting and impossible to achieve. We are always striving to be some fictional character in a book-of-the-month club selection—the perfect parent, the loving spouse, the beauty queen, the entrepreneur, and everyone's best friend. When your age surpasses the speed limit, you like yourself with all your delightful imperfections. Join me as we let our freak flags fly.

1

When You Can't Remember Shiitake

Yes, life didn't turn out exactly as you had planned. The kids aren't brain surgeons, there is still a mortgage on your home, and the brochures for Tuscany are finally in the shredder. Prince Charming looks more like Santa Claus than the football hero you married, and when you glance in the mirror, your mother is staring back at you. It's enough to make you want to cry in your doughnut and fill that empty hole. Tiny Tears, please remember to appreciate all the little things...

You still have all your teeth, and you are solely responsible for giving your dentist his yearly vacation.

RIP to all the high heels you have ever owned. Your Carrie Bradshaw shoes have a new home, Goodwill.

Driving at night is still an option. Yes, it's true that you've slammed into a few curbs, dinged some bumpers, and knocked out one stop sign, but who hasn't?

The Weight Watchers card is finally in the garbage. At last, you are OK with being ten pounds overweight...um, fifteen pounds overweight.

You've stopped plucking your eyebrows; most of your lashes fell out when you went on Medicare. The only part of your body that still needs to be waxed is your mustache.

The social calendar sitting on your desk is filled with invitations: Monday, rheumatologist; Tuesday, dermatologist; Wednesday, cardiologist; Thursday, lab work; and Friday, margaritas.

Braces, college tuitions, and weddings are finally paid off, and the kids really *do* appreciate all you've done for them. Spend that Social Security check any way you like and buy that can of beans… Go hog wild!

Your mailbox is overflowing with letters and postcards. You're happy people still remember you. The local funeral home invites you weekly for coffee, doughnuts, and cremation options. AARP only sends you one letter a month now; they've finally given up.

You are thrilled that your television has a rewind button and closed caption. You can almost understand what's happening on *House of Cards.*

Think of all the times you've held your tongue and been sugary sweet. Take the filters off and let it rip. Everyone will shake their heads, make excuses for you and say, "Ignore her. She's just old, really old."

Please don't mistake me for a Little Mary Sunshine who is trying to paint you a rose-colored world. There are a few minor things you won't be grateful for, like when you can't remember shiitake. The shiitake part begins when you can't find your cell phone. (The phone has a mind of its own and jumps from room to room without any advance notice.) You are forced to use your home phone to call your cell phone to discover where in the heck you put the #$%^&* phone. You run around the house, listening for the ringtone; the culprit is lying under a pile of clothes in the laundry room.

A few months later, you can't find your eyeglasses. This is a grave predicament because you are blind without your trifocals. The kitchen drawer contains fifteen pairs of emergency Walmart readers that are always on red alert. This strange malady spreads like wildfire; you can't find your sunglasses, grocery list, remote control, and your favorite earrings. Your family becomes weary of playing hide-and-seek. They purchase a red basket for you. Their instructions are stern and implicit. "Keep all your valuables in this basket and never deviate from this plan."

You do try, at least for a while, to be organized. Dutifully, all your significant papers, gadgets, and gizmos are neatly placed in the basket. Gradually, the basket becomes a receptacle for Christmas cards, last year's tax return, and a half-eaten bag of jelly beans. In Texas, we like to say, "You can lead a horse to water, but you can't make it drink."

Currently, I have only one blue shoe. (The matching shoe is lost somewhere in Charlotte, North Carolina.) My expensive trifocals are floating around the Kohl's parking lot, and I can't find the receipt for my pants that need to be returned to Dillard's. With three sets of car keys, four sets of house keys, two remote controls, and more glasses than an optometry shop, I am coping fairly well. Forgetting things can be a bummer, but there is always a silver lining. When you start forgetting things, you tend to forget the bad stuff, too. OK, maybe I am a Little Mary Sunshine.

2

Bathing Suit Shopping and Other Traumatic Events

Nothing in the world can strike fear into the heart of a woman more than shopping for a bathing suit. It ranks right up there with a home invasion, mice, wrinkles, and the lone gray pubic hair. Because no one likes to be traumatized, swimsuit shopping is delayed indefinitely.

Our excuses are endless; I need to lose ten pounds, get a spray tan, and my all-time favorite: I need to lose my baby fat. (Of course, the baby is now three years old and even he looks embarrassed when you go to the pool.)

Trauma or no trauma, the time had finally come for my dreaded shopping excursion. With a much-needed tropical vacation staring me in the face, I *had* to get a new bathing suit or change my itinerary to the North Pole.

Off I went to T.J. Maxx, Kohl's, and Dillard's; I grabbed suits in sizes ranging from six to twelve off the rack. I would try the diabolical garments on later that evening in the privacy of my boudoir.

After I was fortified with a tumbler of merlot, the fashion show began, then ended with me calling my therapist. Surely that woman in the mirror couldn't possibly be me! The culprit must be the cheap garments. If a bathing suit had to be purchased, it would be the best one I could find.

The next day, I arrived at a snazzy bathing suit boutique called the Little Shop of Horrors. The shop reminded me of a Parisian bordello. The décor was red and gold with several crystal chandeliers hanging from the ceiling. There were no chairs, only red velvet chaise lounges. Several ladies were sipping champagne in crystal flutes while the manager fawned over them.

I must be in the wrong place, I thought as I ran for the door. A leggy brunette with impeccable makeup cut me off; I stopped dead in my tracks. "Hello, my name is Victoria, and I will be your bathing suit consultant today. How may I help you, dear?"

Is there such a thing as a bathing suit consultant? Do they go to college and get a degree in intimidation? Don't you just *hate* it when people call you "dear," "dearie," "honey," or some other equally condescending term?

"Victoria," I say, "I'm looking for a real change. Something that will make me look thinner, younger, vibrant, beautiful, and sexy wouldn't hurt, either."

"A black one-piece will suit you nicely."

"No, absolutely not, Vicky," I said, downgrading her to Vicky. "I want *color* and something different."

Vicky peered at me through tortoise-shell glasses that looked better than my Walmart readers. After a pregnant pause, she spoke once again.

"Let's see, we have the tankini hipster swim bottom, the halter swim top, the halter tankini, the high-waist swim, blah, blah, blah..."

"OK, I want...um, a yellow tankini. That's the ticket!"

"Yellow? Now that's an interesting choice for you, dear. I'll be right back."

Ten minutes later, I was naked and afraid, cowering in the dressing room and wishing I was anywhere but in the Little Shop of Horrors. Miss Vicky returned with the requested yellow suit with no less than three sizes for me to try on. In a few moments, the new improved me would be unveiled to the world.

"Dear, I thought it best to let *you* decide what size you are. Here is an eight, ten and twelve," Vicky said with quite a condescending air.

It didn't seem that long ago that I had been a size eight, so I started there. The size eight never made it past my knees. I struggled to get the damnable contraption off my body. It felt like a boa constrictor was strangling me.

Maybe a size ten would work better. With sweaty determination, I pulled, huffed, puffed, and yanked on the suit until it was finally on. Ever so slowly, I turned around and looked in the mirror.

Ever heard of the silent scream? The yellow color that I had wanted so desperately made me look jaundiced like I was in the last stages of liver failure. It slowly dawned on me that suddenly I bore a striking resemblance to Big Bird minus the feathers. Undoubtedly, this was a Halloween "fun house" mirror.

Then I heard Vicky speak, "Please come out of the dressing room, dear. We are *all* waiting to see how you look."

Goody, I couldn't wait to have an audience for my unveiling. I cracked the dressing room door open and handed Vicky the three yellow suits. Without a word, Vicky took the three suits from my hand and replaced them with a one-piece black swimsuit.

Damn her! I thought.

Yes, it was a vast improvement because I no longer looked pregnant, but I was not going to *even* look at Vicky and give her the satisfaction. I would march right up to the cash register, pay for the suit, and go home. Vicky stood at the cash register in all her smug glory, with her hands placed on her slender hips.

"I see we chose the black one after all, didn't we, dear? And now, that will be one hundred ninety-five dollars. Would you prefer cash, credit or debit card?"

Was I having an out-of-body experience? Had I lost my hearing? Had she said $19.50 or $195? Because my trifocals were at home on the kitchen counter, I was blind as a bat, and of course, I hadn't read the price tag.

A million thoughts ran through my head. How quickly could I sprint out of the store or limp with dignity on my bad arthritic knee? Suddenly, a mysterious blue light blinded me. It called to me, "K-Mart shoppers, there are blue light specials on aisle eighteen."

With my head held high, I marched out of the store without the bathing suit. After all, Alaska or the North Pole might still be the perfect vacation.

3

Lady Parts

I had just finished my second cup of coffee when I happen to glance at my calendar: "Annual GYN checkup, 2:30, Dr. Henry." It wasn't yet eight a.m., and I was already having my first anxiety attack, thanks to my irrational fear of doctors. Today my lovely plans would have to be scrapped, as I had completely forgotten about my appointment. I wouldn't be going to the Olive Garden for lunch and the senior movie matinee. Instead, I would have to shower, wash my hair, shave my legs and armpits, and exfoliate my bear claw feet—a major project that would take all morning.

By the time I arrived at Dr. Henry's office, I was frazzled. The nurse called me back into her cubicle to do some lab work. I reminded her that I hate needles, especially ones that go into my arm. I get very woozy at the site of blood, particularly mine.

She jabbed the needle into my arm. I'd barely recovered from that ordeal when the nurse directed me to jump on the scale. The last time I jumped on anything was a decade ago.

I gingerly climbed upon the scale, and what did I see? A heinous number appeared, one that would have sent Kelly Ripa into cardiac arrest. "Oh, that can't be right!" I yelled.

I quickly threw off my sweater, belt, scarf, jewelry, and I was just starting to unzip my pants when the nurse pulled me off the scale.

Next on the agenda was my blood pressure. The nurse squeezed the life out of my arm and surprise, my blood pressure was high.

The decathlon continued because now I had to pee in a cup. I tried to explain to the nurse that my bladder is very shy and sensitive, and it doesn't respond well to commands. After sitting on the throne for ten long minutes, my bladder capitulated with a dribble.

The nurse led me back to the exam room and told me to take off all my clothes and put on a pink paper gown that would fit Barbie.

"Please leave the gown open in the front, and the doctor will be in shortly," the nurse ordered.

I sat on the exam table feeling exposed, and waited as the long minutes ticked by. During my vigil, I looked at all the artwork on the walls, consisting of pictures of the female anatomy in graphic detail, which was *exactly* what I did not want to see. Why couldn't Dr. Henry pop for a fake Renoir or a poster of Johnny Depp?

I looked down at my little pink gown, and everything was exposed for the whole world to see. I told myself to meditate and think of something gorgeous, like a beach in Fiji with Johnny Depp.

While trying my hardest to meditate, I spied the metal stirrups at the end of the table. I started panting; they looked like a medieval torture device. I had cotton mouth, and sweat was rolling down my face like I was a heroin addict in detox.

I had to escape this place, but I couldn't leave without saying anything. Last year, I'd told the nurse that my dog was hurt before running out. Maybe I should tell the nurse that my house was on fire or that I'd left my wallet in the car?

The nurse walked in before I was finished plotting. "Nurse, I just got an awful phone call. It's my cat..."

She frowned and shook her head. "The doctor will be here any minute, and *you* aren't going anywhere," she said.

Thanks, Nurse Ratchet.

The infamous Dr. Henry strolled in. He had a big ole grin on his handsome face. He acted like he was thrilled to see me. We talked about kids, grandkids, Tom Brady, politics, and the Dallas Cowboys. I knew Dr. Henry thought this would make me relax and feel like we were on a faux date at a garden party. Instead, it was a date with Dr. Frankenstein.

"Now, let's scoot your bottom down to the very end of the table," Dr. Henry said ever so sweetly.

I moved an inch.

"More," he said with a tone to his voice that I didn't appreciate.

It took all my willpower, but I moved another inch.

He grabbed my legs, and he pulled me the rest of the way.

How RUDE!

I needed to think of something *fast*. "Umm, *stop!* I gotta go, and I mean right *now*. I promise I'll come back; it won't be like last time."

Dr. Henry ignored my plea and proceeded to give me the dreaded Pap smear. By the time he got around to my breast exam, I had transported myself to an alternate universe.

Finally, Dr. Henry spoke. "Well, Debbie, everything looks fine to me. Before you leave, I wanted to take a moment to thank you for being my patient for the last twenty-five years."

"Dr. Henry," I said, "what are you talking about? You aren't retiring, are you? You absolutely can't retire. You certainly don't expect me to start seeing a *new* doctor at this stage of the game? I don't know if you realize it, but I don't do well with this sort of thing and…"

"Yes," he began after a short pause, "the entire staff knows *all* about you. But, no, I am not retiring. Normally, I don't see patients after the age of sixty-five because Pap smears aren't necessary anymore. Of course, if you have any problems, you can always come see me."

"Dr. Henry," I said, "is this your way of saying that at age sixty-five, I am officially *closed for business*? I wish you would have told me that last year because I would have had a *fire sale!*"

For once, Dr. Henry was at a loss for words.

4

Jason, the Cable Guy

It was an emergency. No Internet service!

My left eye began twitching. I told myself to calm down and watch a little television. Then I could deal with calling my internet company, which to me was a fate far worse than waterboarding.

I grabbed my life support, also known as my remote control, and aimed it right at the television.

Gasp, it's not working! I raced into my bedroom, and my other television wasn't working either; my heart was pounding. *God, am I having a heart attack?*

Being cut off from the *universe*, my only consolation was that Baylor Hospital must have cable.

When you live alone, television becomes your new family; you become the star of your own reality show. Every evening David Muir on *ABC News* and I talk about the latest unfolding political drama. He and I often disagree and currently, we aren't even on speaking terms.

In the evening, *Entertainment Tonight* commands the conversation with stories about my favorite celebrities and their juicy scandals. Even though *Entertainment Tonight* hasn't done a tell-all special on my vices, I must confess, I need a twelve-step program for binge-watching; it's bad to the bone, but I love it.

My transgressions include watching all of the following: *Breaking Bad, Stranger Things, Bloodlines, Sons of Anarchy, Shameless, House of Cards, Better Call Saul, Suits,* and now, *Rectify*; I need coffee, doughnuts, and a sponsor.

I drank a glass of *vino* and called the cable company. This is like slamming your head in a car door repeatedly. After spending thirty minutes on hold with canned music dulling my senses, I finally heard a perky little voice. Before I could give "Miss Perky" my litany of complaints, she needed the following vital information: phone number, account number, passcode, address, birthdate, and blood type.

Forty-five minutes later, I finally unloaded my litany of complaints. Miss Perky, who was suddenly not so perky anymore, gave me a long sigh and said, "Hold please."

Several minutes later, Miss Perky returned with the long-awaited news. She could send a repairman tomorrow, no later than 3:00 p.m.

Though both of my eyes twitched wildly, I remained steely calm. I explained to Miss Perky that this was a *genuine* emergency, and tomorrow was impossible. I knew the cast of *Rectify* was going to be worried sick because I hadn't tuned in!

Miss Perky had the sheer gall to inquire about the nature of my emergency. How to explain? My only hope was that she loved TV as much as I did.

"I hope you can understand that I only have *one* more show in the second season of *Rectify*. I need to know what happens to my poor Daniel, who is in prison for twenty years for a crime he didn't commit. I am desperate to know if Tawney will leave Ted Jr. and hook up with Daniel after he is paroled." I took a long pause before continuing, "Miss Perky, I must have my television fixed today."

Miss Perky said the cable guy would arrive tomorrow by three.

I paced around the house like a caged lion staring at the television, willing it to start. I cleaned out the kitchen and ate everything with granulated sugar in it. Suddenly, I had a light bulb moment... Target!

I ran, grabbed my car keys, and drove like a bat out of hell.

I entered the hallowed halls of Target and dashed over to the television section. There, I pretended to look for a new TV. I asked a clerk if he could demonstrate the different types of sets for me.

He smiled and started blabbering about each television's widgets and gadgets. I feigned interest as long as I possibly could, but the clerk was getting on my last nerve.

"Honey, can you please see if you can get the series *Rectify* on one of these sets? I would prefer season two, episode ten."

It was the most depressing ride home *ever.*

All I could think about was how many hours it would be until the cable guy arrived.

The next day, I was like a wild animal stalking its prey. I kept peering out the window, looking for the cable guy as the hours slowly ticked away. My blood pressure soared higher and higher.

Finally, the cable truck rolled into my neighborhood, but it stopped at the wrong house! I bolted out the front door like Superwoman in a cape and slippers. I ran down the street chasing the truck. "Woo-Hoo, I'm over here! This is the house you're looking for!"

The truck pulled in front of my home and out popped the cable guy. "Hi, I'm Jason."

They have to be kidding!

I swear, Jason was twelve and in the throes of puberty.

Upon closer inspection, I saw the colorful tattoos adorning both his arms; so he must have been a teenager. Regardless, this child was incapable of screwing in a light bulb, much less fixing my many problems.

Instinctively, I commanded Jason to sit down because we had to talk. While he squirmed on my sofa, I explained all the reasons I hated his company. He nodded patiently while desperately looking for an escape route; I was beginning to like this child.

He looked a little scared and asked my permission to go out in the garage and look around.

Don't you just love it when a kid is so polite? Jason must have a good mama.

After a solid hour, Jason was still scratching his head. "I might have to go get some parts, but I could come back tomorrow with my boss."

Oh no, he didn't just say that!

"Honey, you just need a cold drink. How about I fix you a tall glass of sweet tea?"

Jason went back outside with his tea, while I kept my fingers crossed. Thirty long, painful minutes passed and not a peep from Jason. Then he finally spoke.

"Lady, I could try something here, but I am not sure it will work."

"Jason, do you remember the children's story *The Little Engine That Could*? The story is about a little locomotive who struggled to get up a steep mountainside. The little locomotive never gave up and kept saying, 'I think I can, I think I can'...Now go back to work because I think you can!"

Jason went back outside with his head hung down. That surprised me after the pep talk I had given him.

Young people don't appreciate anything, do they?

If I didn't do something fast, Jason would bolt. Of course, we all know the way to a man's heart is through his stomach. I whipped up a batch of chocolate chip cookies so fast that even Betty Crocker would have been impressed.

The aroma of fresh-baked cookies infused the air with its deliciousness. The doorbell rang loudly. There stood Jason with beads of sweat rolling down his face and his shirt soaking wet.

"OK, lady, I think everything is working now."

Like magic, the television was finally working and so was the Internet. Unfortunately, my phones were still dead. Jason tried to reassure me.

"It should take about twenty minutes for your phones to reboot. I need to go because I have five more calls to make this afternoon."

Jason wasn't going...*anywhere.*

Maybe, I had seen Kathy Bates in *Misery* one too many times.

"Jason, come on in and have some cookies that I just baked."

It works every single time. I threw Jason's shirt in the dryer and shoved cookies down his throat. His mood rapidly improved.

"Jason, while we are waiting for your shirt to dry, let's watch *Rectify.*"

"Oh, my mom and I have already watched it," he said.

Before I could stop him, Jason told me how season two ended. All bingers know that being a "spoiler" is about the *worst* offense there could possibly be. I quickly sent the spoiler on his way and tried to recite the Serenity Prayer.

5

How to Train Your Trainer

I stared at the number on my scale in total disbelief. A number that simply couldn't be accurate—blinked back at me. *My body needs a complete overhaul!*

I did a quick self-evaluation; my thighs applauded when I stood up, my love handles had cleavage, and my arms flapped like they were about to take wing. Yikes! I had failed countless times, trying all sorts of crazy diets ranging from the Paleo to Jenny Craig. In fact, Jenny and I are such personal friends that we even exchange Christmas cards.

Jazzercise, yoga, Pilates, and a disastrous spin class had made not a dent in my appearance. It took one broken toe and a pulled back muscle for me to banish group exercise from my life *forever.* But much to my surprise, some much-needed inspiration happened that very evening.

While watching *America's Biggest Loser* on television, I became fascinated by how the contestants literally transformed overnight with the help of a good trainer. My goodness, some of them had lost a hundred pounds in just a few short weeks. Why hadn't I thought of that before? I needed a sweet trainer who could make magic happen without a lot of work and no sweating, please. Maybe, what I wanted was a magician. I made an appointment the next morning at my gym.

I crawled out of my warm bed, wanting to do *anything* but go to the gym. I had two cups of coffee, a hot shower, and I got dressed. Luckily, my son works for a sporting goods company and sends me athletic wear; at least I looked the part. My appearance should certainly count for something.

I arrived at the appointed hour, looking like a total jock and feeling proud of myself. I was finally taking control of my life. I marched up to the front desk and had a long conversation with Ed, the manager, about his three trainers.

"Ed, I need someone who likes working with older adults and who can get quick results, like before Christmas."

Ed laughed real loud (I certainly wasn't trying to be funny) and said he had three trainers that I might like: Jim, Nancy, and Tyler.

I ruled out Nancy immediately because she looked like a no-nonsense kind of girl, and that would never work with my sassy nature and snappy repartee.

Jim wasn't suitable either, because he scared the bejesus out of me. He looked like the Incredible Hulk with muscles bulging out everywhere. He had a tattoo of a cobra curled around his neck which didn't help matters.

And then there was Tyler…young, handsome, and sweet looking…perfect for little ole me.

Ed got on the loudspeaker. "Tyler, to the front desk."

Up walked Tyler with a big grin on his face, and he shook my hand. I already loved this kid, until sweet cheeks said he charged eighty dollars an hour. I nearly fainted and found the nearest chair to collapse in.

OK, self, I know it's a lot of money, but you are worth it. (I love to talk to myself, don't You?)

I signed on the dotted line and tried to envision how the new, improved me would look on Christmas Day.

Tyler asked me what medical conditions I had.

"Tyler, is this part of my eighty dollars? Son, that question will take all day for me to answer. I have bad knees, a wonky back, high blood pressure, high cholesterol, low thyroid, and osteoporosis. Do you want me to continue?"

"Um, I think I understand you aren't in the best of shape. Moving right along, we need to weigh you, take your measurements, and see how much body fat you have."

"Tyler, let's skip that part and concentrate on getting me into a size eight by Christmas," I replied.

"This isn't the way it's done. We need a starting point so we can see how much progress you are making each week," Tyler stated rather sternly.

There was so much *wrong* with that statement. Where do I begin? First, there weren't going to be *weeks* involved because I could only afford three sessions. I knew what my starting point was. I looked B-A-D, and I don't mean badass.

With my hands on my hip, I said, "Tyler, we are skipping that part and moving on down the highway."

Tyler looked deflated.

We walked into the workout room, and all the machines looked ominous, and everyone was grunting and groaning. Had I walked into Dante's *Inferno*?

"Let's warm you up first. Jump on the treadmill, and walk a mile at a brisk pace," Tyler said with exuberance.

He is so naïve isn't he? I don't do brisk anymore.

Suddenly, Tyler started acting crazy. He pushed the speed on the treadmill up to three and a half miles an hour. All of a sudden, my feet were flying, and I was hanging on for dear life.

"Tyler, turn this damn thing off right now, and I mean it!"

When I could finally breathe again, I asked Tyler how far I had run because my waist did feel smaller.

"I think it was point two miles. You might do better on the elliptical machine. All you have to do is hold on and push the pedals."

That sounded like a much better option for me, and I was pleased to see that Tyler was finally listening. The elliptical looked futuristic and scary. Tyler hoisted me up on the machine and yelled, "Push the pedals hard, harder…harder."

"Tyler, this is ridiculous. Get me off this contraption right now."

Tyler looked exasperated, but he pressed on. He showed me different exercises—squats, lunges, and sprints. He asked me if I wanted to try any of them.

"No way, José," was my response. All hope was not lost because I spotted an exercise machine that I thought I could actually master.

"Tyler, let's try that machine with the TV."

"OK, that's called a recumbent exercise bike. I want you to concentrate on pedaling and maintain a certain speed."

Ignoring Tyler, I sat down all by myself, which should have impressed the crap out of him. "Tyler, show me how to get the Food Network on this machine."

"I want you to concentrate on pedaling, not the Food Network," said Tyler with quite a bit of irritation in his voice.

I started pedaling and watching television. *Beat Bobby Flay* was on, and it was *very* intense. A chef from Brooklyn was trying to take my Bobby down. The more exciting it got, the less and less I pedaled. I felt a sharp tap on my shoulder.

"Lady, can I use the machine if you are just going to sit there?"

Well, excuse me! I guess I forgot to pedal…

I found Tyler slumped in a corner. "Our hour is almost over. Let's walk around the track to cool down." I didn't dare tell Tyler that I didn't need to cool down. As Tyler and I strolled around the track, I had to ask him one last burning question.

"Tyler, how much weight do you think I lost today?"

Tyler's eyes glazed over, and he gave me a blank stare. "How does three pounds sound to you?" I couldn't hide my sheer disappointment. I had been hoping for five pounds.

During our stroll, Tyler began opening up about his love life, of course, with my prodding. He and Amber had been dating six weeks, and everything had been great in the beginning. Now she was always busy when he called, and she was acting weird. How could he get this relationship back on track?

"Tyler, think about it this way. You are the substitute teacher filling in until her dream man shows up. Dump her! It's a hundred times better to be the dumper than the dumpee."

"You are so right, and it's funny I never thought of it like that. Thank you and I really can't charge you for today because we didn't do anything. Today is totally on me if you promise *not* to come back."

I had been right about Tyler all along. He was adorable.

"Tyler, I'm going to tell every last one of my friends about you."

As I walked out the front door, never to return, I could still hear Tyler screaming, "*NOoooooo!*"

6

Peanut Butter and Jelly Roll Blues

Why is it that the phone only rings when you are in the shower? With water dripping everywhere, I grabbed the phone and barked, "Hello!"

Ryan, my neighbor, was shouting at me. His wife was in labor, and he needed help with his kids, who were still asleep. There was a distinct disadvantage to being the only one in the neighborhood who was retired. I was the "go to" person for letting plumbers in, picking up packages, and now, babysitting.

I arrived at Ryan's house in five minutes flat. Ryan bore a marked resemblance to Casper the Friendly Ghost and Allison, his wife, was doubled over with labor pains. I whisked them out the door and drank my first cup of coffee.

At eight thirty, I woke up Morgan (seven) and Marley (five) and explained that their new baby brother should be arriving shortly.

With the kiddos sleepy-eyed and in their dinosaur pajamas, we drove to my house. I got the children dressed and poured them bowls of Captain Crunch.

"Oh, our mom doesn't *ever* let us eat sugary cereal," said Morgan.

This was going to be a problem. I had never been a fan of oatmeal unless, of course, it was in a cookie, and I didn't have any eggs.

"Today, I want you to walk the gangplank, Morgan, and enjoy the Captain."

After breakfast, I told the kids that they could play outside because it was a gorgeous day.

Marley said, "Did our dad arrange a playdate for us?"

"What's a playdate?" I naively asked.

The children tried their best to explain to me the *intricacies* of playdates. They had to be kidding, right? When did we stop letting kids play outside by themselves? Parents, in years past, never had to worry about their children because stay-at-home moms who were on duty around the clock patrolled the neighborhoods. When my kids were growing up, I would give them a rope, jacks, a tin can, a ball, and a piece of chalk, and I wouldn't see the whites of their eyes until the dinner bell rang.

We marched outside with a piece of green chalk in my hand. I drew a hopscotch board and explained the complexities of the game. After round two, my right knee gave out, but the kids played for a solid hour. We advanced to the game of jacks. I am a jacks player from way back and demonstrated the ins and outs of taking down your opponent. Morgan declared this was a baby game and wanted to play video games on his iPad, which had become an appendage.

"Morgan, if you can beat me at jacks, you can play video games to your heart's content." Morgan easily mastered the onesies, but the foursies…well, that was another story.

We headed inside for lunch and I fixed PB&Js and some milk.

"What's that brown stuff on the bread?" Marley asked.

Then Morgan piped up, "We don't drink milk. Our mom doesn't let us eat anything with peanuts because she is afraid we might be allergic. Can we go to Chipotles? We like their chicken bowls."

Were these kids pulling my leg? My entire family existed on peanut butter and jelly sandwiches for years, and dining out was a rarity.

"Today, kids, we are walking on the wild side, so dig in, and if you want to put your sandwich in a bowl, be my guest."

The kids took their first tentative bites and then their second bites. They declared they didn't like it, but they ate it anyway. I guess peanut butter and jelly is an acquired taste.

Just about that time, Ryan called from the hospital. Allison was going to have an emergency C-section, so he wouldn't be home anytime soon. I started to need a mini vacation, which in "senior speak" means a nap.

"Hey kids, I think we need to rest for a while."

"We are *too* old to take naps," both of them replied with shocked looks on their little faces.

"One is never too old to take naps. You both go lay down, and you may read or play video games."

I put a quilt over them and closed the door. An hour later, I woke up in a nervous jerk. The house was deadly still. Were the kids OK? Had I been derelict in my babysitting duties? I cracked open the doors to the guest room; my two visitors were sacked out. I calculated I had just enough time to make myself a quick cup of coffee and regroup.

That afternoon we made orange Popsicles with some orange Kool-Aid that I had left over from VBS (vacation bible school) complete with Popsicle sticks. I had impressed the kids with my ice cream wizardry. We moved on to homemade chocolate chip cookies. Most of the raw dough was gobbled up before the cookies got in the oven. We were on a sugar high when Ryan called to let us know that their new baby brother had arrived. He asked me if the kids could stay for dinner and promised that he would pick them up before eight.

As evening approached, I lit the fire pit in the backyard. We roasted hot dogs and marshmallows and stuffed them down until we couldn't eat another bite. The kids wanted to know if they were going to spend the night with me. I assured them that their dad would be arriving shortly to take them home. Was that a look of disappointment I saw on their little faces? We captured fireflies and put them in mason jars, and the kids were fascinated at how they lit up the backyard.

"Can we play one last game?" Morgan begged. Yes, Morgan was finally going rogue.

Ryan's car drove up while we were racing around the backyard playing "olly, olly, oxen free." Ryan heard all the commotion and he asked us what was going on. How does one explain to a millennial what going "old school" is all about? Ryan thanked me profusely, and I got bear hugs from the kids. I put my jacks in Morgan's hand and told him I expected a rematch. I heard Morgan and Marley ask Ryan if they could come back tomorrow. Uh-oh...

7

Plausible Deniability

The Urban Dictionary defines plausible deniability as a condition in which a subject can safely and believably deny knowledge of any particular truth that may exist because the subject is deliberately made unaware of said truth so as to benefit or shield the subject from any responsibility associated through the knowledge of such truth.

When Dr. Sully insisted that it was time for me to have a colonoscopy, I had trouble breathing. This procedure sounded horrifyingly invasive and painful and like something I needed to avoid at all cost. Dr. Sully reassured me I was making a very big deal over absolutely nothing.

"You'll have medicine to take the night before the procedure, and the next day will be a piece of cake. We'll give you some good drugs, and it will be over before you know it. If Katie Couric can do it, so can you," Sully said with a grin on his face.

Damn him! Dr. Sully knew the way to get me to do anything was mention a celebrity. Yes, I did faintly remember Katie's television special on getting a colonoscopy. Katie had looked calm and like her usual bouncy self when she told America that there was nothing to this procedure. A blatant case of fake news!

A few weeks later, the pharmacist handed me a quart bottle of a thick green liquid. He must have noticed the dubious look on my face.

"It's not bad and it tastes a lot like lemonade. Be sure to drink the entire bottle *before* your procedure," he instructed.

Is he in cahoots with Sully?

The pharmacist reminded me that tonight was Halloween and the trick-or-treat candy was on sale. Great! On top of everything else I was dealing with, I wouldn't be able to do my yearly candy gorge.

At the appointed hour, I took my first sip of the green goop. Jeez, it tasted more like battery acid than lemonade. I held my nose and took a few sips. The liquid in the bottle hadn't gone down at all! Katie Couric had made it looks so easy. At that precise moment, my brain began debating…

I can't do this.
Yes, you can. You have to.
No, I don't!
Do you want colon cancer? Do you?
Nooo.

At five thirty when the doorbell rang with my first trick-or-treaters, I couldn't wait to see them in their cute costumes. I chatted with my neighbors and gave the kids mountains of Kit Kats. As I closed the door, my tummy started to rumble slightly. I strolled into the bathroom.

The clock indicated that it was time for round two of the devil's brew. Like a good soldier, I held my nose and drank some more. My stomach began cramping up just as the doorbell rang. I tossed the kids candy without even commenting on their adorable Halloween costumes and sprinted for the bathroom.

I barely kept the third dose down. When the children rang the doorbell, I cracked the door open and threw candy at the little kids. They could fend for themselves just like I was doing. After the fourth dose, I left the candy outside and bolted the door.

I drug a pillow and blanket into the bathroom and surrendered. The alarm clock chirped at five, and I drug myself off the floor. Gazing into the mirror, a woman who looked like she had been hit by a diesel truck stared back at me. I mustered up the strength to brush my teeth and wait for my daughter. My girl walked in and said the words that almost got her a knuckle sandwich.

"See, Mom, it wasn't so bad."

We arrived at the hospital, and I made a beeline for the bathroom, my new favorite hangout. The ordeal was almost over, and I tried to look on the bright side. This experience was like a Hollywood cleanse that my insurance company had to pay for. I knew I had dropped ten pounds because I felt light as a feather.

As promised, the procedure was painless and I got a great nap, too. My doctor dropped by to tell me everything looked fine.

"Debbie, see, there was nothing to be afraid of, was there?"

"Dr. Sully, have you ever had a colonoscopy?"

"Oh no, heaven sakes, I'm only forty."

"So until you have had one, Sully, you are guilty of plausible deniability."

8

Waldo and Me

I had no intention of getting a dog; I really didn't. Yes sir, no dog for me. For the first time in years, I had absolutely no responsibilities. My children were grown. I was retired from work, and I had left my ex-husband in the rearview mirror. I was finally free at last, or so I thought…

Like most good stories, let's start at the beginning.

I was on my way to pick up a catering order from Jason's Deli when I noticed a crowd had gathered in front of the local pet store. The Humane Society was there with all kinds of dogs to adopt.

I walked by briskly but not before noticing the saddest dog I had ever seen. The dog looked like a stuffed animal that should be sitting on the shelf at FAO Schwarz. He was a little ball of yellow fur with big brown eyes poking out.

"Not today, buddy," I said as I marched into the deli. Of course, my order wasn't ready, so I had to sit and wait.

I peered out the window and watched as families adopted dogs and children jumped for joy.

Oh, surely my sad friend had found a good home by now.

I grabbed my Reuben sandwich and headed back to the car, and I almost made it home.

Yes, OK, I admit it. I drove back to Jason's. I *just* had to make sure my "sad dog" had found a good home.

The Humane Society was closing up shop for the day and putting the "sad dog" back in their truck. He stared at me with the most miserable look on his face.

"Wait," I yelled.

Yes, I became a parent once again. *Sigh*! I named him Waldo.

When Waldo was introduced to his new surroundings, he suddenly had a brand new attitude. Gone was the "poor pitiful me" persona, and it was replaced by total swag.

This braggadocios behavior was unlike anything I had ever seen before; he was an imposter!

I quickly showed Waldo the ropes: where his food was, where he could go potty, and where his new sleeping arrangements were; he listened and placated me that very first day.

The next morning, I jumped out of bed because I knew Waldo would have to go to the bathroom.

"Come on, Waldo. Let's go potty." Waldo had a look of total disdain on his face. He marched outside, did his business, and stood by the door waiting for me to let him in.

When I opened the door, he glared at me. I just knew what he was thinking. "Don't ever talk baby talk to me again, and I will let *you* know when I need to relieve myself."

I put Waldo's breakfast of dry kibbles down before his majesty; he didn't eat one single bite. Instead, he looked at me, and I swear I heard him say, "*Really?*"

I hate to admit it, but Waldo intimidated me. We shared a waffle, bacon, and egg. I learned he liked eggs over easy.

The next day, I needed to find a good vet for my new friend. I figured he needed shots and a good checkup. Mysteriously, Waldo knew just where we were going; he flatly refused to budge from the car.

We had a wrestling match; I barely won.

The price of victory was steep; I was not going to be defeated by a mere six pounds. With a pulled back muscle, scratches on my arm and a bad attitude, we limped into Dr. Campbell's office.

The nurse called Waldo's name. I drug him into the exam room. It took Dr. Campbell, his nurse, one assistant, and a partridge in a pear tree to hold Waldo down for his shots. After that ordeal, Dr. Campbell said, "You know Waldo has not been N-E-U-T—."

Waldo snarled, bit Dr. Campbell, peed on the table, and gave me the meanest look ever.

"Ah, let's hold off on that for now, Dr. Campbell." I was going to have to find a new vet who spoke Waldo's language.

Waldo wasn't speaking when we got home, and he no longer trusted me. I expected to see a horse's head on my pillow that very night. It took two days of me cajoling Waldo with treats, ice cream, and car rides before he wagged his tail my way.

See, the way to Waldo's heart was car rides; he was a born road dog. He could hear the jingle of car keys from fifty yards. He insisted that he was my new travel companion, and he behaved quite nicely in the car. Unfortunately for Waldo, I couldn't always take him with me.

If I backed the car out of the driveway without Waldo riding shotgun, he would glare at me from the front window of our home. I would return home to find my expensive high heels tossed around the house, newspapers shredded, trash cans overturned, and Waldo would have peed on the floor, never in the same place twice. Waldo and I needed couples' counseling.

Dog walking is supposed to be an excellent exercise for man and beast. I bought Waldo a sturdy collar and leash, and I thought we would stroll through the park, throw a Frisbee, and have some fun; we never made it to the park.

Waldo sniffed and peed on every plant and blade of grass he found and drug me behind him. We walked about twelve feet and called it a day. There are some battles you just can't win, and from that point forward, we went where Waldo wanted to go. After four months, we finally made it to the park.

Waldo and I found our stride together after the first couple of years, just like newlyweds eventually do. I talked to him all the time and he'd answer in Waldo's language: eye rolling, tail wagging, barking, glaring, and growling.

He was always overjoyed to see me at the end of each day, and I felt the same way about him. I would come rolling in the house with my litany of complaints: the traffic sucked, I had a headache, I needed a vacation, someone at work had royally pissed me off, and the list went on and on.

Waldo would patiently listen. He'd nod his head in total agreement, but then, he would cut me off, cold turkey.

He would march over to his leash as if to say, "*Girl*, you need some fresh air and a new attitude."

Off we would go.

Waldo was a genius. By the time I got home, I felt refreshed and was in a much better mood.

On our first Halloween together, Waldo and I debated right up until the witching hour what costume he would wear. I was surprised that Waldo had a passion for acting; I bought him three outfits with hats to match: Captain Waldo Sparrow, the Dark Dog Knight, and Spider Dog.

We chose the pirate costume, and I must say that Captain Waldo Sparrow was the greatest swashbuckler I had ever seen. When the trick-or-treaters arrived, Waldo ran to the door with his puffy purple pantaloons and a foam sword dangling by his side. He pranced around in his costume for the kiddos, and he loved all the attention.

I had no idea that he had aspirations to be an actor. I fostered his talent for dramatics on Easter, the Fourth of July, Valentine's, and Christmas, but he would have none of it.

Halloween was his gig; actors can be so temperamental.

But Waldo wasn't all bluster and bravado. One night, I discovered his Achilles heel—a Texas rainstorm.

The wind howled while buckets of hail pelted the roof. Streaks of lightning flashed across the room, and a loud clap of thunder made me shudder.

My brave little man was suddenly doing his version of shake, rattle, and roll. I grabbed Waldo and threw him in bed with me, but that didn't do the trick. I explained to him that he had nothing to worry about. It was just rain. He remained unconvinced.

That first storm, we watched the sun come up together, sitting on the back porch. I smiled, thinking that all-nighters hadn't happened to me in a very long time...

Waldo was the most selfless person I ever knew.

One night, I came home from work and felt awful. Waldo took one look at me and said, "Uh-oh." I crawled into bed with a raging case of pneumonia. I lay in the fetal position for eighteen long hours without moving. Waldo stayed right next to me, and he didn't move a muscle.

Waldo never barked for water or food or even indicated that he needed to go outside. Worried about Waldo, I finally made myself get up, and Waldo breathed a big sigh of relief. Life slowly returned to normal for Nurse Waldo and me.

The years quickly passed, and Waldo's energy and vitality waned with old age. After many visits to Dr. Campbell (yes, he did become fluent in Waldo speak), he was diagnosed with ALS. Waldo had trouble walking and eating which broke my heart. Waldo, in his usual fashion, fought the good fight. When Waldo told me that it was time to go, I knew better than to argue with him. He went peacefully to sleep in my arms like he had so many times before. Good night and safe travels, my precious Waldo…

After several weeks of me suffering from depression and heartache, the doorbell rang one morning. It was my neighbor Sue, and she was mad as a hornet's nest.

"My dog, Stella, is P-R-E-G-N-A-N-T by Waldo!"

"Are you sure it's Waldo's?" I asked. "Waldo was so sick that I can't believe he could do that."

"Do you remember when you took Waldo to the dog park six weeks ago? He was fooling around with my Stella. I saw it with my own eyes."

Oh, I couldn't stop laughing. Leave it to Waldo to make a final curtain call and have the last laugh on everyone.

"You'll have to excuse me, Sue. I need to run to the store and get a new doggie bed, leash, collar, and puppy food because Waldo Jr. will be arriving shortly."

Part Two

In-Laws, Outlaws, and the Un-Familia

My dad was a staunch Roman Catholic who dreamed of becoming a priest. Mother was a southern belle who thought going to the First Presbyterian church was more of a social event than a religious experience. My brother, a bluegrass musician, was a practicing Buddhist, and I married a Jew. I never knew at dinnertime *if I was supposed to make the sign of the cross, wear the Star of David, or chant The Five Reflections. Trust me, I know about hilarious, dysfunctional, and highly entertaining families...*

9

Lake Wicky Wacky

Over the years, various friends have shared with me hair-raising stories about their family reunions. I find these stories to be a great source of amusement. A reunion is anywhere the entire clan has gathered—a wedding, funeral, or a family vacation. We all love our families but put the circus clowns in one room...its cray-cray. Four words that I tell anyone planning to attend a clan gathering... *proceed with extreme caution.*

The sweltering, lethargic days of summer make the idea of a family reunion sound like fun. Some knucklehead plans it, and everyone agrees to attend. All the attendees envision it will be like the Walton's or the Adam Sandler movie *Grown Ups*. Everyone will be laughing, playing, roasting marshmallows, frolicking in the lake, and singing "Kumbaya." Family reunions always have a cast of characters, and each character has a role to play in the melodrama.

The Drones: They are the ones who do all the heavy lifting. They cook all the meals, wash and dry dishes, and continually pick up after everyone. The Drones abhor confrontation, and they would rather be galley slaves than out in the fray.

The Queen and King Bees: While residing in their own unique universe, Bees are oblivious to any chores or tasks that need to be done. While the Drones are cooking and cleaning, the Queen Bees have their heads buried in their iPads, looking at clothes online or texting the world. The King Bees are watching sports and ignoring everyone else. The Bees participate in planned activities only if they are held at gunpoint.

The Organize: This person likes to have a master plan for the entire group. The Organizer enjoys telling others what time to get up, go to bed, eat breakfast, and turn the television off. He or she has an agenda for everyone and pity the fool who doesn't follow the agenda. The Organizer orchestrates everything from bike rides to scavenger hunts.

The Opinionater: God bless their pea-pickin' souls, the Opinionaters want to give you their views on everything under the sun. Their lecture series includes, but are not limited to politics, religion, and the kind of cereal you should eat. If you dare disagree, they will beat you into submission until you surrender.

The Showstopper: This person *must* be the center of attention and in the spotlight at all times. During the reunion, you can count on him or her to upstage you. If you have read a great book, the Showstopper has read six classic novels. If you have gotten a promotion at work and want to toot your own horn, the Showstopper has had dinner with Prince William. These characters change the subject in a flash and bring it back to themselves every single stinking time.

The Inebriater: There is always one in every family who overindulges and then feels free to say or do whatever he or she pleases. Ironically, this person has amnesia the next morning.

The Peacekeeper: This person runs interference better than a pro linebacker and tries to keep everyone happy and in a good mood. It's a juggling act that would make Barnum and Bailey proud.

Now that you know the cast of characters, let our story begin…

Aunt Sue, the Organizer, rented a huge house at Lake Wicky Wacky and invited the entire clan. Sue e-mailed everyone a list of all the events that were, of course, preplanned: a luau, charades, a scavenger hunt, and a family picnic. Sue calculated the expenses to be just under four hundred dollars per family. Ouch! In addition, each family was instructed to bring dinner for twelve for one night.

After receiving Sue's letter, I announced at dinner that in three short weeks we were all going to Lake Wicky Wacky for our family reunion. At once, my darling children began their litany citing reasons they simply could not and should not be required to go. I put a halt to their diatribe after ten painful minutes, and they stormed off in a massive pout.

A week later, after reality had kicked in, the kids ask if they could bring all their electronic equipment to the lake. I said, "Sure, why not?" I didn't have the courage or heart to tell them there was no Wi-Fi at the lake. I was a coward.

Three weeks later, we arrived at the lake for the long-awaited reunion. Eight family members stood in the cabin's driveway to greet us. Everyone was waving and hugging it out because it was good to be together once again. It took the kids a split second to realize there was no Wi-Fi. I was now on America's Most Wanted list.

By the time we unloaded the car and put everything away, we were beginning to wonder when the fun part was going to start. Everything went smoothly until dinnertime. Aunt Sue read from her master list.

"Connie, you are assigned dinner tonight. What are we having?"

Connie, the consummate Queen Bee, said she didn't get around to it, what with work and everything. Without a drop of remorse, she immediately went back to reading her romance novel. Connie's pronouncement threw Mary and Evelyn, the Drones, into a complete dither. They huddled together and hurriedly decided to fix pasta with pesto. Pots and pans began flying around the kitchen.

While waiting for dinner, Uncle Frank commenced with his lecture series on politics. Uncle Frank, the Opinionater, proclaimed that President Trump *would* make America great again and Fox and Friends was the best show on television. Julie, the Peacekeeper, cringed. We were the lucky ones because we had *two* Opinionaters *in* our family, Dave and Frank, and they held opposing views on everything under the sun. Uncle Dave yelled at Frank that Trump was the Antichrist and Bernie should be our president. Julie felt she must intervene, interjecting that she just loved *both* the political parties equally. Julie's nonsense left both Uncle Frank and Uncle Dave livid and the rest of us speechless. We said a silent prayer that tomorrow would be better.

The peacefulness of early morning at the lake can be ethereal. I was enjoying every minute of the quietness until I heard a loud commotion downstairs. It sounded like people were arguing and it wasn't even seven o'clock yet. I ran down the stairs, and the culprit was Fox News. Uncle Benny, our elder King Bee, had the volume on the television turned up so loud that the walls were vibrating. He had a death grip on the remote control, and he was not going to give it up without a fight. Julie, our Peacekeeper, asked Benny to "pretty please, with sugar on top, turn off the TV." It was waking up everyone.

"No, sir, I watch Fox News first thing in the morning because I want to stay informed," Benny shouted with the utmost irritation in his voice. What Benny forgot to mention was that he needed to stay informed all day, every day and well into the night.

Mary and Evelyn, our resident Drones, broke the land speed record and dived into the kitchen to make blueberry pancakes to appease everyone. When Connie, the Queen Bee, asked if the pancakes were gluten-free, I had to restrain the Drones.

The rest of the day was fun, and yes, we all participated in the water sports that Sue arranged. Even the kids were having fun jet skiing and swimming. Everything was rolling along nicely, until the incident with Uncle Charlie, the Inebriater. Uncle Charlie was always the life of the party, until he wasn't anymore. Charlie's breakfast consisted of Bloody Marys with beer chasers.

Charlie was guzzling his fifth beer when our cousin Ann walked out on the deck. I was the first one to declare that Ann was crazy to wear a bikini, but she was a tried and true Showstopper. Ann was divorced, passed her prime, and sixty pounds overweight. She greeted everyone and then, with great flair, dropped her bathing suit cover. There, for the whole world to see was an itsy-bitsy, teeny-weeny little pink bikini. Ann slowly waddled into the water with the pink bikini radiating in the sun.

It was at that precise moment that Charlie decided to tune up. "Hey, is Ann pregnant? Who's the poor guy?"

Everyone lost their flippin' minds. Ann cried, Charlie laughed, Sue suggested a potato sack race, and Mary and Evelyn passed snacks around. Dave and Frank argued over Charlie, and Connie finally looked up from her iPad to ask what all the fuss was about. Dinner was eerily quiet, as we all were silently counting down how many more fun-filled days until we could go home.

The rest of the week was fairly uneventful, as we all adjusted. Fox News and I woke up together each morning, and we all learned how to shout over the television. Evelyn and Mary finally handed over the kitchen duties to the rest of us because they were exhausted, and finally they started having fun. We all pretended Connie was a ghost and that suited her just fine. The kids and I participated in all of Sue's planned activities, and we actually had fun and got some great selfies, too! Frank and Dave took over the front porch and argued about everything under the sun, and they loved it. Ann put her pink bikini away, along with her diet, and she began to enjoy herself.

On the morning we were leaving, I snatched the remote from Benny and ordered him to take the trash out. Out of the corner of my eye, I spied Connie's sacred iPad. Connie would get her iPad back after she cleaned the entire kitchen. Being the commander in chief can be exhausting.

The kids packed up, and it was finally time to say goodbye. We all hugged and thanked Sue for organizing everything. She said, "No problem," and then announced she was planning a ski reunion for this winter. Oh snap!

When we got in the car, I looked back at my "chocked full of nuts" family standing on the front porch. My eyes filled with tears. "Hey, Mom, what's wrong?" the kids asked.

I said, "Not one single thing."

10

Larry, Queenie, and Me

The idea of a road trip began innocently enough. Frank, my neighbor, dropped by and mentioned that he had an overnight business trip to Fredericksburg the next day. My blunder was introducing him to my cousin, Queenie, who was my houseguest. Frank, trying to make polite conversation, asked Queenie if she had ever been to the Hill Country. She said that she had not but added, "I would just *love* to see it!" Frank halfheartedly invited us to join him the next day. Queenie accepted for both of us before I could slap my hand over her mouth. Frank announced that we would be departing at 0700 the next morning.

I must digress and tell you a little bit about my travel companions. Frank is a retired Special Forces colonel who doesn't suffer fools kindly. Queenie, on the other hand, is pure cotton candy. She's an authentic "Alabama belle" who never met a stranger, and the word *schedule* is not part of her vocabulary.

Our road trip begins…

7:00 a.m.: When the rooster crowed, Frank was banging on our front door. Queenie opened the door in her pajamas and invited Frank to come in and have some coffee.

"Um, I thought we established that our departure time would be at 07:00 Frank said quite sternly.

"Oh, Frank, why I haven't even had my second cup of coffee yet, Sugar" Queenie explained.

I flew around the house trying to get us ready to leave, as I knew Frank wasn't a happy camper. Forty-five minutes later, we handed Frank four suitcases, two pillows, and a *National Inquirer.* Frank had a backpack and a baseball hat.

Frank announced that our ETA in Fredericksburg was readjusted to 1300 (1:00 p.m.) We would have to make up for the forty-five-minute delay. He asked us several times if we needed to use the restroom before we left, which Queenie thought was highly personal. Away we went!

8:20 a.m.: Queenie *just* had to pee; the second cup of coffee was the culprit. Frank was irritated and mumbled that we were losing *even* more time.

9:45 a.m.: Queenie spied the Czech bakery and pleaded with Frank to stop just for a teeny, weeny minute because she was starving. Thirty long minutes later, Queenie returned with a bag of pastries, three cups of coffee, and two postcards. She tried to cajole Frank with coffee and a sweet roll, but he wasn't having any part of it.

On the road again...

10:45 a.m.: Queenie screamed, *"Stop the car."* Frank swerved the car over to the side of the road.

"What the hell is wrong with you?" he yelled.

Queenie jumped out of the car.

"Just *look* at the bluebells!" Queenie exclaimed.

Frank's left eye began twitching, and his face turned bright red. Unfortunately, Queenie was oblivious. She popped open her iPhone and started taking pictures like she was the paparazzi chasing Brad Pitt.

"Frank, stand next to Deb over by the bluebells. Now sit next to each other in the grass, hold a bluebell in each hand. That's it. OK, now let's take a selfie. Isn't this fun? Now, Frank, I want one of you all by yourself."

Frank was fuming. I saw sparks flying out of his eyes, which was very scary stuff. But wouldn't you know that now I had to pee too! It was a crisis. I hope to this day no one saw me squatting by the tire, mooning the world.

11:00 a.m.: The car was deadly quiet as Frank sped down the highway. I whispered to Queenie not to say *one* word until we stopped for lunch. Gradually, I cajoled Frank into talking about his army career, and the ice started slowly melting. He regaled me with old war stories, and he even cracked a smile. I chatted with him about battles, weapons, and armed combat, anything to improve Frank's mood.

"Frank, what would you do if you were in a life-threatening situation and you had no weapons?"

Frank gave me a sly smile and announced that he could kill someone with just a ballpoint pen. I was fascinated and repelled, all at the same time. Captain Cranky was in a good mood once again. Frank even suggested that we stop for a *quick* lunch in Salado. He was trying to make amends and gave us a new ETA of 1500 (3:00 p.m.) for Fredericksburg. I breathed a huge sigh of relief.

11:45 a.m.: Lunch at McCain's Bakery and Café, Salado, Texas. While waiting for our table, Queenie struck up a conversation with a couple from Wisconsin, Lou and Marty. They were laughing just like old friends who had known one another for years. Queenie made the fatal mistake of insisting that they join us for lunch. For over an hour, we were entertained with the history of cheese curds. Frank never opened his mouth once, which was a very ominous sign. He kept staring at his watch, and I knew he was recalculating our ETA. Queenie didn't take the hint. I tried to hurry us along, but she was busy exchanging e-mail addresses and telling Lou and Marty that she was going to send them a friend request on Facebook the *very* next day.

Then the unthinkable happened! Queenie spied a book about Hillary Clinton in Lou's jacket.

"Oh, honey, you better not let Frank see that book! He will stab his ballpoint pen *right* in your eye! You just wouldn't believe all the ways Frank knows how to kill someone!"

Lou and Marty jumped up from the table, looking positively terrified. Frank stormed out of the restaurant with us running right behind him.

1:00 p.m.: We jumped into the car, and no one said a single word. Finally, Frank had to stop for gas. "Ladies, I want to make it crystal clear to both of you that *no one* but me is getting out of the car," Frank snapped.

Queenie just couldn't stop herself. "But what have we done wrong, Frank?"

"Queenie, you can't handle the truth," Frank snapped.

I had to put my hand over Queenie's mouth; I knew she was just going to say *one* more thing. I even passed her a note begging her not to say a word while Frank was pumping gas, but who should appear? You guessed it, Lou and Marty. Queenie rolled down her window with lightning speed.

"Honey, you come over here right this minute. Frank says that I am not allowed to get out of the car."

Marty cautiously walked over.

"Queenie, are you girls all right?" Marty asked.

"Oh, sugar, we are just fine. Frank's just an old, grumpy bear."

Marty casually told Queenie that Jenna Bush's rehearsal dinner was in Salado, and Marty knew exactly where the restaurant was. Now that was the worst thing she could have possibly said! It was like waving a red flag in front of a bull because Queenie adores anything to do with famous people. Before I knew it, Queenie had cracked opened the car door and low crawled over to Marty's car. Away they went...

Frank got back in the car. Thankfully, he didn't notice that Queenie had absconded. I had to stall for time.

"Frank, I don't feel very well. I must get some medicine and use the restroom."

What could Frank say to that? I got out of the car and stayed in the convenience store for as long as possible. As I slowly walked back to the car, trying to think of what I could say to Frank, the renegades drove up.

"See, you didn't *even* miss me, did you? We saw Jenna's wedding pictures, and she was adorable."

I jerked Queenie's arm and threw her into the backseat. Frank started clicking his ballpoint pen...

2:30 p.m.: Queenie slept, and I didn't dare utter a word. She woke up just as signs for the LBJ Ranch came into view. We were both shocked and delighted when Frank wanted to stop. I guess he had surrendered his ETA, or he would have had a brain hemorrhage. The ranch was beautiful, and Frank even got out of the car and took a few pictures. Queenie, trying to make amends, bought us tickets to tour the ranch. Frank just mumbled that we needed to make this a very quick tour.

Absolutely nothing is quick about Queenie. She latched on to our tour guide, and he commented that no one had ever asked him so many questions. The guide casually mentioned that Lady Bird and LBJ were buried at the ranch. Immediately, Queenie asked the guide for directions because she just *adores* cemeteries. She begged Frank to drive us to the cemetery, and she promised she wouldn't ask for *another* thing the entire trip. Unfortunately, Queenie hadn't written down the directions.

Frank drove around and around in circles. Queenie begged him to stop and ask for directions. Frank was having none of that nonsense. Queenie rolled down the window and yelled to anyone she saw.

"Woo-hoo, can you tell us how to get to the cemetery?"

Frank gunned the engine. Dirt and car fumes flew in Queenie's face. She finally surrendered, and Frank, at last, found his way back to the highway.

5:00 p.m.: We rode in silence the rest of the way to Fredericksburg. When we arrived at the hotel, Frank tossed us our room key and stormed off. We unpacked, showered, and had a real heart-to-heart conversation. I told Queenie about her many transgressions that day and strongly suggested we fly home tomorrow for everyone's mental health. Queenie felt remorseful and wanted to try to make amends with Frank by inviting him to dinner.

6:30 p.m.: We knocked on Frank's door, but there was no answer. The door was unlocked and we gently cracked it open. Frank was standing in front of the television holding the remote control like a life force. All the lights in the room were off, and the television was casting an eerie glow over Frank's face. He was watching the movie *Lone Survivor.* Queenie slowly backed away and quietly closed the door.

Even Queenie knows that there are times in life when you just have to wave the white flag.

11

Harriet and Fred, the Uninvited Guests

The week of Thanksgiving seems a lot like football to me because the center snaps the ball, and the game is on! Every single day is filled with a million errands from Christmas shopping to holiday baking. On the Thursday before Thanksgiving, my world turned upside down when I saw Harriet's e-mail.

She and her husband, Fred, distant cousins of mine, would have an overnight stay in Dallas before their trip to Paris. Harriet asked if they could stay with me for just *one* night.

I sat at my computer fuming! If they had enough money to go to Paris, they could certainly afford a lousy hotel room. If I didn't complete my holiday errands, I would have to cancel Thanksgiving, which is as bad as canceling Christmas. I e-mailed them and acquiesced; yes, they could spend *one* night. I have never learned the art of saying no.

I arrived at the airport and patiently waited for Harriet and Fred. Their flight was delayed one hour. When they finally arrived in the baggage claim area, they were missing two suitcases. The missing luggage sent Harriet into a state of apoplexy and propelled Fred into having a confrontation with a poor, unsuspecting customer service agent. After assurances that their bags would be on the next flight, we headed home. I mentally started counting down the hours until they left...Twenty-two hours and six minutes to be exact.

As soon as we pulled into my driveway, Fred wanted to know how much I had paid for my home, as though he were a real estate agent dying for a listing. I took a deep breath and said, "Too much."

Don't you just hate rude people that ask intrusive questions?

I offered my guests some wine, hoping to improve everyone's mood. Fred proceeded to lecture me on wine from California and the Pacific Northwest.

"It's the *best* wine in the world," Fred proclaimed.

I told Fred that wines from Tuscany were my favorite, especially good Chianti. They were far superior, in my humble opinion.

Fred yelled, "Let's just fact-check that, missy."

Fred whipped out his iPhone with lightning speed, and he proceeded to quote *Wine Spectator* like this magazine was the gospel of Saint John. I noticed that Fred kept doing a gyration in the air with his fingers when he wanted to make a point.

"Fred, what are you doing with your hands?"

"Oh, I use air quotes when I want to emphasize a point."

I was dying to show Fred my own "air quotes" that only require one middle finger, and there is no confusion in the message. Harriet could tell that I was getting annoyed, so she tried to cajole me with a hostess gift.

"We brought you a little something and want you to open your gift and put them on *right* now."

To my horror, a pair of neon pink Candies (cheap plastic shoes) stared back at me from the shoebox. Before I could squeak a weak thank you, Harriet revealed that she was the vice president of her local PETA chapter and it hurt her heart to see people wear leather shoes because just think of those poor suffering cows. Oh, for pity sakes. I put the pink contraptions on and took a few painful steps. If only I hadn't thrown out my old *Where the Beef* T-shirt.

Because we were having such a rollicking good time, Fred decided to add to the merriment by getting on his soapbox about everything under the sun. From recycling plastic to making cleaning products, Fred was an expert. Was it possible that I was a POW in my own home? If Fred said another word, I would gladly waterboard myself. Thirty minutes later, Fred finally ran out of steam.

With three glasses of wine under my belt, I served dinner. I had prepared my favorite meal: Texas chili with all the trimmings, cheesy jalapeno cornbread, and chocolate cake with fudge icing. Harriet and Fred exchanged a very odd look.

"Oh dear, I guess we forgot to mention that we have a few dietary restrictions. We are vegans, gluten intolerant, sugar-free, dairy free, and we have peanut allergies."

I couldn't stop myself… I really couldn't.

"Fred sounds like you and Harriet need to go to a hospital more than you need a trip to Paris." I enjoyed my Texas chili while my guest dined on a wilted salad.

Bon appétit everyone!

At last, it was time to call it a night. Fred stopped me at the pass; he needed a few things before he and Harriet could retire for the evening. Did I have a fan? They simply couldn't sleep without one. Did I have allergy-free pillows? Harriet had awful allergies, especially in this godforsaken state of Texas. Did I have a television for their room? It would be impossible for Fred to sleep without CNN blasting in his ear. Did I have a noise machine to drown out the street noise? No. That was my answer to all the above questions. I ran into my bedroom, tossed the pink Candies in the trash, and put a pillow over my head.

The next morning, I woke up thinking that I must have been having a terrible dream. What were the noise and smell coming from my living room? It was still dark outside, and my alarm clock read 6:00 a.m. Did I have an intruder in my home? Blurry-eyed, I staggered into the living room.

Harriet was on her yoga mat doing the" downward dog" pose while the sweet smell of incense permeated the air. New Age music blasted from her iPhone, and my head started to pound. I couldn't deal with Harriet without some caffeine surging through my body. I walked into my kitchen only to find Fred in his pajamas, intently watching CNN.

Fred barked, "We have been up for over *an hour* waiting for you! We've been searching for your decaffeinated coffee."

"Fred, I don't drink decaffeinated coffee, and that's why you can't find any. You early birds can hike to Starbucks if you like. It's about a mile down the road, but I'm going back to bed."

Now I was feeling guilty, damn it! They walked out the door, looking a little bewildered. As Dr. Laura would say, I needed a new attitude. I finally got up at seven thirty, poured myself a second cup of real coffee, and brushed myself off. I only had to make it until four o'clock. My uninvited guests returned from their trek to Starbucks covered in sweat with several mosquito bites. Fred began bellowing as soon as he walked through the front door.

"This is ridiculous to have eighty-degree weather in November. Where we live, it's already cold, and all the leaves are turning. How can you stand it here?"

I must take the higher road for once in my life.

"Let's go out for lunch today. There is a new vegetarian restaurant in Grapevine, and I think you both might like it. After lunch, we should go directly to DFW Airport. With security being so tight on international flights, you want to be there at least three hours ahead of time," I said in the sweetest voice possible.

"Our travel agent told us to be at the airport two hours ahead of time," snapped Fred.

"It's better to be safe than sorry," I replied. "Let's talk about Paris and all the things you should do while you are there. I like to stay on the Left Bank because it feels like the *real* Paris to me. Of course, you must go to the Louvre and take a boat trip down the Seine at twilight. My favorite Parisian bistro is—"

Fred stopped me in midsentence. He began spouting off about all the research he had done on Paris and how he certainly didn't need my help. Fred was a disciple of the travel author, Rick Steve, and he would only follow *his* advice.

"Fred, at least let me help you if you and Harriet get lost in Paris. Just memorize this sentence. '*Je deteste les grenouilles francais.'*"

Fred ordered Harriet to get a pen and copy the phrase down immediately. He was finally listening to me, but unfortunately for Fred, the sentence meant *I hate French frogs*. The French were simply going to *adore* Harriet and Fred.

I had to escape for a little while to keep my sanity in check. I told my guests that I had a quick errand to run and I would be home shortly. I ran to Safeway and did all my Thanksgiving shopping. I called Fred and told him I was running late and to start packing.

Fred and I unloaded three hundred dollars' worth of groceries. Was it my fault that Fred's travel clothes were all sweaty by the time we finished?

"Oh darn, we aren't going to have time for that lunch after all. No worries, there are plenty of restaurants at the airport," I said reassuringly.

We drove up to terminal D and parked the car. I wanted to make very sure that they didn't miss their flight. As we walked into the terminal, I just happened to glance up at the departure board. The flight to Paris had a four-hour delay! I quickly evoked the spirit of David Copperfield and *poof*...I vanished. I did hear a background noise that sounded like Fred screaming, *"Where is sssshhhhhheeeee?"*

12

A Hunting We Shall Go...

Skydiving, an African safari and camping were the last three things on my bucket list. Glancing at my dwindling savings account, it was clear that camping would be the only viable option this year. It was past the time to heed the siren's call, experience the great outdoors, sleep under the stars, and roast marshmallows over a roaring fire.

This was an imperfect plan...

I needed help with my brain child because I didn't know zilch about camping. My son-in-law, on the other hand, is a West Texas cowboy who knows all about the great outdoors. He would be the perfect foil.

My family had just polished off Easter dinner, and everyone was in a good mood. I made sure my son-in-law had two helpings of coconut cake; he was primed for the slaughter.

"I've decided to fulfill one of the last things on my bucket list, a camping adventure. Who wants to go with me?"

Troy, my grandson, piped up. "Gram and I need to go camping! Dad, please, please."

Did I mention how much I love that kid?

My son-in-law, Dusty, shook his head and sighed. "Your grand-mother would *hate* camping."

George, my oldest grandson, chimed in that his dad *did* have camping gear in the garage that was just sitting there. My hero!

"Mom, where do you want to go on this camping trip?" Dusty asked.

I had to think about that for a minute or two. "Let's go where there are tall pine trees and beautiful mountain streams. And the weather can't be cold or too hot. Clean bathrooms like Buc-ee's are a must and hot showers would be glorious."

My son-in-law sighed deeply. "You're talking about the Holiday Inn in Boulder, Colorado."

After much whining on my part, my plan had legs. My nephew Matt, an avid outdoorsman, would be joining us for the camping extravaganza. Our destination would be four hours away at some random campground near Tyler, Texas. For two amazing days, we would breathe in the outdoors and commune with Mother Nature. I couldn't wait to cross camping off my list.

Matt and I arrived at Dusty's as the sun was peeking through the clouds. The boys loaded up the truck with all kinds of manly stuff like fishing gear and tents. Dusty looked at all my luggage and tossed me one scruffy backpack.

"Everything you want to take needs to fit into this one backpack."

We were off to a very rough start. Our wagon train had gone twenty miles when I spied a Starbucks and insisted we stop.

"Nope," yelled the four stooges.

I must have been delusional to go on a trip without another woman in sight. I was outnumbered, but I hadn't surrendered, not quite yet. We finally arrived at a remote campground, and there wasn't one tall pine tree or a rippling stream in sight.

"OK, everyone, grab a bag, and start setting up the tent," Dusty barked out.

"Honey, I need to find a restroom; it's a *real* emergency. Just point me in the direction where the bathrooms are," I yelled.

"Mom, see that bush over there? That's your new bathroom for the next two days." It was a toss-up whether to laugh or cry.

"Did you bring any toilet paper, Dusty?"

He held up a leaf and grinned.

Two hours later, the tent was finally up. It was hotter than blue blazes, and a swarm of mosquitos decided I was a tasty meal. The men went fishing, and I tagged along because there was nothing to do at the stupid campground. As soon as they started fishing, it became too quiet.

"Hey guys, let's play twenty questions," I suggested, hoping to break the monotony.

All the guys said in unison, "Shush."

Fishing is the singular most boring sport in the world, just in case you didn't know.

We returned to our campsite, and the boys were starving. Suddenly, everyone looked at me. My new assignment was chief cook and bottle washer. I was popular once again! The boys got the campfire roaring, and the T-bone steaks came out of the cooler.

Grabbing a black cast-iron skillet, I attempted to cook the steaks. After a severe case of smoke inhalation, one scorched eyebrow, and a big blister on my arm, the steaks were ready.

No one warned me about the inherent dangers of camping.

Night fell and all the stars came out. You know, it's true that the stars are the biggest and brightest deep in the heart of Texas. The five of us sat around the campfire and roasted marshmallows. Just when I had begun to relax and enjoy myself, George asked Dusty a question that would change the course of events.

"I'm scared. Will wild animals come into our tent tonight, Dad?"

Dusty assured him that we were all safe and no wild animals were around our campsite.

Thoughts of wild animals now danced in my head. *What if we get attacked by a wild boar? What if a rattlesnake bites me? What if a coyote grabs me? Why, oh why, didn't I pack toilet paper and Xanax?*

I calmed down and remembered that we still must tell ghost stories to complete our experience. I had a scary story all prepared for the occasion, "The Bloody Finger." Unfortunately, the idea of ghost stories received a speeding bullet from the four snipers. DOA.

With nothing to do and no one to entertain us, the men declared it was bedtime. We walked back to our hot, sweaty, claustrophobic tent, and the boys were snoring in perfect unison within minutes.

Who can fall asleep this early?

I grabbed my flashlight to play level 233 of Candy Crush, but I couldn't concentrate on smashing the candies due to the chorus of snoring. Still wanting a real camping experience, I grabbed my sleeping bag and headed outdoors. Yes, I would overcome my fears and sleep under the stars like an honest-to-goodness camper. I was drifting off when I suddenly heard a noise.

My ears perked up, and I listened intently. Was that a black bear or mountain lion? The sound seemed to be getting closer and closer as my heart raced faster and faster.

My piercing scream woke up the snorers, and they came bursting through the tent.

"I hear a noise," I screeched.

They dragged me back inside that miserable tent and told me not to leave again or I'd be walking home solo.

The next morning, a vote was taken; it was unanimous. We were heading back to the land of air-conditioning, comfy beds, and In and Out burgers. The truck was packed, and we headed toward home, sweet home.

I had an immense feeling of satisfaction that I could cross one more thing off my bucket list. Of course, there was still skydiving hanging over my head. I know exactly what I want for Christmas, tandem skydiving with Dusty. Now that's something that I'll have to work on.

13

A Brother from Another Mother

Once a year, the Dallas Police Department invites family members to do a short ride-along with their loved ones so they can experience firsthand what the police do on night patrol. Paul made the fatal mistake of relaying this juicy tidbit of information to me.

Paul and I aren't related by birth but by the heart. He is my official little brother. I suppose the word "little" is deceiving when describing him. He is six foot four and 250 pounds of solid muscle. He carries a big black gun and would scare the crap out of most people but not me. My Paul is a sweetheart, but like all little brothers, I must make him walk the line. I like to call him *Paulie Parton* (after Dolly Parton) just to remind him who's boss.

We decided to meet at a local restaurant to talk about the details of our upcoming adventure. While discussing the ride-along, I casually mentioned that I had to renew my driver's license. This year I would have to take an actual *driving* test; I couldn't renew my license online. Paul calmed me down and suggested that we go for a spin so he could evaluate my driving skills. He promised not to say *one* word until the ride was over.

As I backed out of the parking lot, a car nearly crashed into us…

"That damn fool wasn't watching where he was going," I shouted.

Paul suddenly looked worried. "You need to start looking in your rearview mirror," he cautioned.

"I thought you weren't going to say *anything*. I can't look in my rearview mirror and straight ahead, too," I screeched.

Paul gave a big sigh and directed me onto the freeway. "You need to turn right at the light…Right, right…Your other right, OK."

"It would be helpful if you would shake your hand in the direction you want me to turn. I can never remember my right from my left, and you know that."

All of a sudden, he was yelling again. "Speed up now, or we are going to be rear-ended," he shouted.

He was getting on my last nerve. "Paulie, I'm not about to go fast with five lanes of traffic, orange barrels, and trucks zooming by us going eighty mph. They can just figure it out and go around us."

"Why do you have one foot on the gas and one foot on the brake? You only need one foot for *both* the gas pedal and the brake." He sounded highly annoyed.

"That makes no sense at all. I need both feet available at all times, Paulie Parton!"

"Get off the freeway now and go back to the restaurant. Why are you speeding up in a residential area? The speed limit is only thirty-five miles per hour!" he shouted.

"For someone who wasn't going to say anything, you've said quite a lot, mister! I am going faster now because I can. There are no trucks to worry about and no orange barrels, silly."

Paul became very quiet as we walked back into the restaurant. He yelled to the waitress to bring him a beer.

"But, Paulie, you don't drink…"

"I do today," Paul said.

One week later, it was time for the infamous ride-along. I had a duffel bag stuffed to the brim with everything we would need—a flashlight, gloves, tape measure, notebook, and a ball point pen. My supplies were perfect for a covert operation.

I arrived at the police station right on time. I was waiting outside when Paul walked up. I was dressed all in black from head to toe.

"It's a little early for Halloween, isn't it? Why are you wearing sunglasses at night?"

I ignored his rudeness.

We pulled away from the station, and Paul droned on about his rules for the evening. "Don't even think about touching my gun, handcuffs, the radio, the keys, the steering wheel, the windows, and never, *ever* speak to anyone I arrest."

Everyone who knows me understands that I am a rule breaker, not a rule follower.

"If I get an emergency call, you can't come. I'll let you out of the car and pick you up later."

Oh no...*he didn't just say that!*

"I will do no such thing. If you get an emergency call, just take me to the nearest Starbucks, and I will wait for you there." Just the idea of leaving me on the side on the road was crazy talk.

All of a sudden, the radio crackled and came to life! We had our first caper of the evening. Paul put the sirens on full blast, and the red lights on top of the patrol car were flashing. Away we went!

Oh, I love being a cop!

We arrived at the crime scene where an elderly man stood in the driveway with two teenage boys. The old man had one of the boys in a choke hold, and I surmised he must be a retired Marine. I wrote all this down in my notebook. Paul would thank me later.

Paul growled at me to keep the windows rolled up, and he warned me to stay in the car. Everyone knows that I am hard of hearing, so I had to roll down the window just a crack to hear what the heck was going on.

Oh my! Paul handcuffed one of the boys and tossed him into the back of our patrol car. He walked over and started talking to the old man and the other teenager. This was my *only* chance to get the real scoop from the boy in the backseat. I had to take the risk.

"Bless your heart, honey, what have you gone and done to yourself? Those tattoos are *awful*, and how many earrings do you have in each ear? Oh, sweet Jesus, what are those silver studs in your tongue? When you are forty, you will be so sorry you did such a damn fool thing to yourself. Now we don't have much time. What's your name? Where do you live? Does your mama know where you are? Tell me your side of the story. I'm listening."

"Who are you, lady?"

"I'm the best friend you have tonight, sonny," I said in my most commanding voice.

The boy looked at me suspiciously, trying to size me up—an impossible task.

"I'm Ace, and I'm innocent. The other kid did it. He's blaming it on me because he threw the rock at the window and tore down the old man's mailbox."

"Ace, look me straight in the eye, and tell me you didn't do it."

"I'm innocent. I swear. It's legit!" Ace cried out.

Paul jumped into the front seat of the car, looking very serious and official.

"Officer Paul, Ace has something he wants to tell you. Go ahead, Ace. It's all right, darling." I was trying to give Ace an infusion of courage.

Paul's neck suddenly turned beet red like he was having a stroke or something.

"OK, dude, I didn't do it; there's been a mistake. This lady said you would take me home and forget about everything," Ace pleaded.

I knew that I was in trouble; I had to fix this mess.

"Now, honey, say you are very, very sorry just like we talked about," I said cajolingly.

"Sorry, man," Ace replied.

Paul suddenly looked mean as a junkyard dog, and it even gave me the shivers.

"Ace, it's a super sweet story, but I pulled your license. Let's see, one DUI and a stint in juvie, that's quite an accomplishment for a sixteen-year-old."

"The other kid did it. I swear." Ace sounded scared.

Paul wasn't buying this sob story. "The other kid cuts the grass in the neighborhood but nice try. Awesome news, Ace, you *are* going home, just to a new home called city jail."

It was a long ride back. When we pulled up to the city jail, I handed Ace a Kit Kat. It was the least I could do for the kid.

Ace looked long and hard at Paul. "Who is she?"

"Oh her...she escaped from a nursing home. I'm dropping her off next." Paul chuckled.

Until next year, Paulie Parton, I promise to do better...maybe.

14

Uncle Henry's Funeral

Funerals are a big thing in the south; they're a command performance, and all the kinfolks, far and wide, must attend. When Queenie called me with the news of Uncle Henry's passing, my attendance in Montgomery, Alabama was required. If anybody but Queenie had called, I would have politely declined and sent a pretty floral arrangement and a sweet card to Aunt Alice Faye. After all, Uncle Henry was eighty-four years old, and by all accounts, he had a good life. But no one in their right mind says no to Queenie, or you'll never hear the end of it.

When I got off the plane, I easily spotted Queenie in the crowd. She was chatting with a bunch of strangers. (You might remember Queenie from "Frank, Queenie, and Me.") Everyone in the crowd looked expectantly at me because Queenie had told them that I was a very famous Texas writer. You should have seen the sheer look of disappointment on their faces when I appeared. She introduced me to all her new airport friends, and then we were off to the races.

Before we went to the funeral home to pay our last respects, Queenie insisted that I just *had* to see the graves of singer/songwriter Hank Williams and his wife. You do remember, gentle readers, that Queenie just *adores* cemeteries, don't you? Our next stop was the capitol and the Museum of Fine Art. Of course, we just had to stop for biscuits, southern fried chicken, turnip greens, and sweet tea.

When we arrived later that afternoon at the Thompson Funeral Home, Aunt Alice Faye was in her widow's weeds holding a full-court press for all the visitors who had come to pay their final respects. Alice Faye insisted that everyone stand in line to view Uncle Henry's corpse. The thought of seeing a dead person caused me to have a terrible case of hives and made my head spin. No matter how much Queenie insisted that I stand in line, I wasn't budging.

Aunt Alice Faye walked over to me, placed an iron grip on my arm, and carried me over to the mahogany coffin.

Queenie could move with lightning speed, and she had tattled on me to Alice Faye.

I cracked open one eye and saw all two hundred pounds of Uncle Henry laying in repose. His old, faded Crimson Tide sweatshirt barely covered his potbelly, and his Bama baseball cap covered his bald head. In the coffin were some of Uncle Henry's favorite things: an autographed picture of Coach Bear Bryant and a bottle of Jack Daniels, his lifelong companion. I laughed so hard I was literally shaking. Queenie had to drag me out of the funeral home with tears running down my face. I was told later that Queenie spread the news that I had a nervous condition.

I pleaded with Queenie to let me stay at my hotel and skip the funeral, but even after the laughing fiasco, she was having none of it. She gave me one of her "calm you down" pills, and off we went to the funeral.

As soon as we stepped out of the car, the summer heat hit me smack-dab in the face. The sweet smell of all those funeral flowers made me slightly nauseous, too; attending this funeral was a very bad idea. Queenie instructed me to sit down in the closest pew and only think happy thoughts.

Aunt Alice was running the show like Bob Fosse in *A Chorus Line*. She had all the people who would pay a final tribute to Uncle Henry lined up with herself being last, for the most dramatic effect possible. While I was sitting there counting down the minutes until this ordeal was over, I noticed a woman in a low-cut white dress enter the church. She had platinum-blond hair and too much makeup for a lady past her prime. I pointed her out to Queenie, and she turned in her seat so fast she almost got whiplash.

"Why, who is that? I have never seen *that* woman before, and I know absolutely everybody in town. Why, she looks like a floozy," Queenie exclaimed. She began quizzing everyone in our pew, and soon the church was buzzing with questions about the mysterious woman.

Alice Faye was the last person to expound on the virtues of dear old Uncle Henry. He was the love of her life, a great father, a Rotarian, a kind soul, a great friend, a humanitarian...blah, blah, blah. I was just starting to drift off when the mysterious woman stood up.

"Alice Faye," the woman cried, "Hank loved *me* best, not you. Hank and I have been lovers for the last twenty years, and I miss him, too!"

An eerie silence fell over the congregation, and 150 people collectively gasped. The choir director grabbed her baton and signaled the organist. The choir burst into the loudest version of "Amazing Grace" ever recorded by man or beast.

The congregation stared in shock as Alice Faye marched off the podium, clicking her heels. She headed straight for the floozy. The blond interloper got the message and bolted for the door. After all, no one puts baby in the corner, especially if it's Alice Faye.

Queenie leaned over and whispered in my ear, "Now, aren't you glad you came to Uncle Henry, or maybe I should say Uncle Hank's, funeral?"

Sweet Home Alabama...

Part Three

Star Struck

*F*ormer First Lady Nancy Reagan believed in astrology. Her astrologer, Joan Quigley, advised Mrs. Reagan on many important decisions during her time in the White House. Yes, Nancy trusted the stars and their alignment in the galaxy. I'm a lot like Nancy; I believe in the stars, too! The only difference is mine are movie stars!

My obsession with movies stars began in 1955 at the ripe old age of ten. The Empire Theater in Montgomery, Alabama, was the culprit. Every Saturday morning, kids poured into the theater for the *kiddy matinee. For a mere thirty-five cents, I could watch endless cartoons, serial movies like* The Adventures of Captain Africa, *and a double feature film. I became addicted at ten, and I'm still shooting up on…Hollywood.*

15

My Achy Blakey Heart

I had a wild, sexy dream last night that I never wanted to end. I was on Blake Shelton's pontoon boat in Broken Bow, Oklahoma. We were drinkin' ice-cold beer, and he was playing his guitar and serenading me with "God Gave Me You." It was like I was the *only* girl in Blake's world.

He confided in me about Miranda (Lambert), and he is *over* her, which was such a huge relief. Still, there was the tiny issue of Gwen (Stefani), his reported new love. Crimes of passion are allowed in dreams, so I threw Gwen overboard. In dreams, anything goes, particularly if it involves men I like.

Blake wasn't my first love, not by a long shot. I have had many love affairs in years past, and they all ended disastrously, like the one I had with Johnny Depp.

The trouble with Johnny is that he never listened to my advice. I warned him repeatedly about marrying Amber Heard, the blond hussy. No, he forged ahead and married her anyway. If he had only listened to me, he might *not* have thrown a cell phone at her head and saved himself millions of dollars in alimony. And what about poor Vanessa Paradis, the mother of his children, who he simply forgot to marry? Vanessa and I are *over* you; do you hear me, Johnny?

The Ryan Gosling love affair is still seared in my brain. He's been such a disappointment. While being interviewed on *Entertainment Tonight*, Ryan was quizzed about what kind of woman he finds attractive.

"Anyone that looks like Eva Mendes," is what that fat bastard said.

The last time I looked in the mirror, I bore no resemblance to Eva. We both have eyebrows, and that's as far as it goes. I had to banish Ryan from dreamland *forever*.

My last entanglement before Blake was with Adam Levine (Maroon Five). I knew Adam was a long shot, but I like a good challenge.

Adam is hands-down drop-dead gorgeous, no doubt about it. It was no surprise that *People* magazine voted him the Sexiest Man Alive. His eyes are ocean blue, and he has the bone structure of a Greek god. I love his full head of black hair, but I do scold him when he dyes his hair blond or shaves his head.

Here was the dilemma with Adam. He is a little too metrosexual for my taste. I know that he waxes, gets mani/pedis, facials, and he is better groomed than I am. Besides that, I can't imagine being stark naked in front of Adam. (I allow myself to be slightly risqué in my dreams.)

I love you, man, but I can't be with a man who wears smaller pants than I do.

Yes, I have come full circle; Blake is my one true love, for *real*. He is everything that I have been looking for and more. He is tall, muscular, and he outweighs me by one hundred pounds. Hallelujah! He has that boyish country charm, and you just know that he is full of shiitake. Can you hear me squealing?

I know what you naysayers are thinking. Blake drinks too much. He likes women *way* too much and will break my achy Blakey heart... *Not listening.*

See you in my dreams, cowboy.

16

Someone's in the Kitchen with Ina

It was time for me to throw an awesome party and be the hostess of the century. To orchestrate such an event, I needed inspiration and expert guidance. I was going to the mountaintop where Ina Garten reigned supreme as the *Barefoot Contessa* on the Food Network.

In case you aren't personal friends with Ina like I am, let me give you the backstory. She lives in a gorgeous home in the snobby East Hamptons with a garden that would rival Central Park. Jeffery, her husband, is always happy. He compliments Ina on just about every single thing she does, which makes me wonder if he is an alien from outer space. Jeffery works in New Haven and comes home only on the weekends.

Think how many divorces could be prevented if we only had to see our spouse two days a week? Brilliant, Ina!

To prepare for my upcoming party, I watched Ina closely as she planned and executed a dinner party for eight in thirty minutes flat. I quickly grabbed a pen and took copious notes because this looked easy.

The first thing on Ina's agenda were linens. Her linens were every color of the rainbow, pressed and neatly stacked in rows like she had a Chinese laundry in her basement. Ina chose crisp white linens for her party, and she grabbed a white tablecloth to demonstrate how to set up a bar cloth with straight edges. Of course, she had china and crystal glasses that were every shape and size imaginable. What a hostess! But Ina did enlist help for her party: Ted, Dennis, and Ross. These men were all extremely handsome, creative, talented...and a tad gay.

Oh, why don't I have friends like that?

Ted, the florist, arrived first at Ina's home with gorgeous arrangements of white roses and hydrangeas in lovely crystal vases. Dennis, the lighting expert, came next with his crew. Before Ina could even blink an eyelash, twinkle lights were in all the trees, and luminaries lined her garden walkway. The backyard looked like a fairyland, and Ina hadn't lifted one pinky.

The last to arrive was Ross, Ina's bartender for the party. Ina and Ross discussed which signature cocktail should be served at her soirée. Ross mixed several concoctions for Ina to taste, and she chose French 75. Every fabulous party must have a signature cocktail; it's the gospel according to Saint Ina.

Ina prepared her gourmet dinner in thirty minutes flat. I timed her. She whipped up potato pancakes, rack of lamb, and apple crostata. Ina was smiling and laughing the entire time while she was cooking and naturally, her kitchen remained immaculate.

If I follow her simple directions, I will be the most famous party giver ever!

The day of my party, I woke up early because it was time to execute Ina's plan. I opened my linen drawer and found the following: four plastic placemats, a Christmas tablecloth, and a runner with an Easter Bunny on it. The only ten matching plates I had were from Albertsons, and one of them had a chip.

I needed help; EZ Rentals to the rescue. Two round tables (Ina says these tables are best for conversation), ten chairs, and tablecloths were charged to my beleaguered MasterCard.

I needed to recruit volunteers for my party. Bob, my neighbor, liked to drink more than anyone I knew; he should be an expert on cocktails. Bob happily agreed to make his "signature cocktail."

Next, I contacted Tony, who was studying to become an electrician. He would be perfect for the light show. I hoped he wouldn't disappoint and would give me the *wow* factor, just as Dennis had done for Ina.

It was time to tackle Ina's thirty-minute meal. I read the first recipe and cringed. Potato pancakes are a lot of work, what with shredding the potatoes and frying them, and think of all those grease splatters! I agreed with Ina that everyone *does* love potatoes, but what if I ditched the pancakes and substituted potato chips with onion dip? No one can just eat *one* potato chip, can they?

The star of Ina's culinary masterpiece was rack of lamb. A lot of people don't like lamb (just ask my son-in-law). Maybe I should pick something more "taste bud friendly," like hamburgers with sesame seed buns. Who doesn't love a good burger?

The last thing on Ina's list was her *pièce de résistance*, apple crostata. Even though it sounded yummy, I would have to peel all those apples and make pie dough. Mrs. Smith's frozen apple pie is hard to beat so, Mrs. Smith won again.

The day of the party was chaotic. The rental people arrived with all their paraphernalia and almost collided with the florist. Still, everything was coming together at last, just as Ina had promised. The only snafu was the unbearable heat and the pesky mosquitos.

Tony would be arriving shortly with his light show, and my party would finally be Ina Garten perfect. I hoped he came early so I could take it all in before my first guest arrived. As I was getting dressed, I spied Tony in the backyard.

"Hey, when do I get to see your light show, Tony?"

"Close your eyes and don't you dare open them until I say so. *Now open your eyes.*"

Gasp!

Tony had placed a huge floodlight that would have been perfect for landing a 747 aircraft in my backyard. My yard looked nothing like Ina's fairyland but more like a runway at DFW Airport.

Sue and Bob arrived with the signature cocktails. Bob opened his cooler with great panache and behold...a case of Coors! Turns out, Bob was a huge Denver Bronco fan and believed there is but *one* beverage on earth worth drinking.

A vote was taken to move the party inside; the heat and mosquitos were killing us. Besides, we were all nearly blinded by Tony's floodlight. From the safety of my air-conditioned kitchen, we all admired how fabulous the backyard looked, all lit up so brilliantly. Many had seconds on the burgers and most stayed past midnight. My party was a roaring success.

I hope with all my heart that Ina won't be disappointed when she reads this. Ina, I love you gal, but this is how people from Texas do the East Hamptons...Yee-haw!

17

To Sir Paul with Love

Have you ever had a dream that seemed so real that you can't decide if you are asleep or awake? That's exactly what happened to me the other night. I tossed and turned for hours. I tried counting sheep, thinking happy thoughts, and humming Beatles songs. I started thinking about Paul McCartney...

My love affair with Paul began in 1964 when the Beatles first appeared on *The Ed Sullivan Show*. Paul, John, George, and Ringo were electrifying, and I was one of the millions of girls screaming at home while watching them sing "I Want to Hold Your Hand." Paul was the devilish one with his long bangs and sexy smile. He and I grew up together over the years, but the timing was never right. Paul married three women, but I never lost hope that one day I would be number four. I'm awesome that way.

Now was my chance. Paul was finally coming to Dallas in concert, and we could, at last, connect. For once in my life, I didn't care how much a concert ticket cost. I gleefully gave Ticketmaster my maxed-out credit card. Three hundred dollars later, a concert ticket was in my sweaty palm.

The night of the concert I couldn't afford a limo, so I had to drive myself. I fueled up my old Camry and headed out to the show. Just call me the lucky one because I had the pleasure of driving at rush hour. Cars rushed past me like Dallas was suddenly being evacuated. Had I missed a tornado warning? Some friendly drivers speeding by even offered me the one-finger salute. Frazzled, I arrived at the venue with white knuckles gripping the steering wheel.

The guard at the gate barked, "Forty dollars to park." I handed Mr. Wonderful four dollars. (Even in my dreams, my hearing is lousy.)

"Forty dollars or move it," he growled.

I handed him some plastic and prayed that he, of all people, wouldn't steal my identity.

Once inside the concert hall, I realized I had made a ghastly mistake! I hadn't eaten anything before leaving home. After more than two hours without eating, I got even more light-headed than usual. Calculating that my expenses had already reached three hundred and forty dollars, I had to be careful with my food purchases.

I fought my way to the concession stand pushing others out of the way. They call it a "concession" stand for a reason. You have to "concede" all value of money and every lick of common sense you have ever had to pay the prices they demand. The throngs were pushing their elbows into my back; I had to decide quickly. I purchased a small Coke and one hot dog.

"That's twenty dollars," yelled the concession genius. I would have to call *Guinness Book of World Records* in the morning and notify them that I had eaten the most expensive hot dog on record.

I walked over to the next kiosk where vendors were hawking an assortment of items with Paul's picture plastered on everything from baseball hats to T-shirts.

Oh, I wanted a T-shirt so bad I could taste it, but it was forty dollars. Did I dare?

With Paul's picture hugging my chest, I felt pretty sassy. I noticed a long serpentine line with women talking a mile a minute. This required an investigation.

"Hey, what's going on? Did someone get hurt?"

"No, this is the line for the restroom," the woman replied.

Why it's called a "restroom," I will never know. I mean really, who would want to rest in that place?

How could I get past the throng of women because I really should tinkle before the show starts?

"Look everyone. It's Paul McCartney!" I yelled, pointing.

Jackie Joyner would have been so proud of how quickly I sprinted past everyone who was craning their necks looking for Paul. I locked myself inside that stall with a smile on my face.

Juggling my million-dollar snacks, I "mountain climbed" up to my seat in the nosebleed section. This had to be an egregious error. After forking over three hundred dollars for a seat, shouldn't it be in the front row and include a lap dance from Paul? (Please don't tell Blake Shelton I said that.) The usher wasn't listening as I explained that a mistake had obviously been made and I should be sitting in a floor seat.

"Lady, you are in the right section. Floor seats start at eight hundred dollars." He stated that fact like it was perfectly natural for a sane person to pay eight hundred dollars for a seat. This would be my last concert, end of story!

Suddenly the lights dimmed, and the crowd quieted down. Sir Paul rose like the Phoenix appearing on the stage in all his magnificent glory. The band began to play, and I began to swoon. My sweetheart sang "I Want to Hold Your Hand." OMG *that* was *our* song! He remembered!

The crowd was on their feet, cheering and fist pumping; Paul had to calm us all down. He grabbed his guitar and began to sing "Let It Be." This song was about his mother, and when a man gets sentimental about his mom, I start weeping.

Sir Paul sang all the songs I love—"Lady Madonna," "Hey Jude"—and he ended the show with "The Long and Winding Road." Everyone held up lights while swaying to the music, and we all sang along with him. I felt so close to Paul and all the other people in the room. What a night! I was in heaven, and this particular heaven was worth every single penny I spent.

When the concert was over, I was the last one to leave the stadium. I wanted this night to go on forever and ever. I knew it was time to go home when I was mistaken for a member of the cleaning crew. Slowly, I found my way out of the building and began looking for my car.

You know, I can never remember where I park.

Lost, alone, and wandering around the parking lot at midnight, I suddenly heard someone shouting at me.

"Wait up, luv. It's me, Paul. I saw you tonight, and I had to say hello."

The moment had arrived for me to say what had been in my heart all those years. "Paul, I have loved you with a passion since I was sixteen, and I love every single song that you have ever written. You are brilliant." (This is how I act when I am playing hard to get.)

Paul winked at me and gave me his adorable smile. "Luv, let me sing you a little song."

Paul dropped to one knee, grabbed his guitar, and sang "Baby, I'm Amazed."

After that fabulous serenade, I was going in for the long-awaited kiss. I put my arms around him, and when our lips were almost touching, the alarm rang.

Reality bites the big one...

18

Eat, Love, and Hallucinate

The other night I watched the movie *Eat, Pray, Love* for the last time, I swear! I've watched that movie so often that I know the dialogue better than Julia Roberts. When Javier Bardem says to Julia, "Darling, it's time," I swoon.

What is it about movies that mesmerize me when the subject matter is about women running away from home? Take for example *Thelma and Louise*. I watched that movie numerous times, and no, it wasn't just because of Brad Pitt. I think the part I liked best was when Geena Davis leaves her husband's dinner in the microwave and she and Susan wave *toodle-oo*. Oh, I can't count how many times during my marriage that I wanted to toss dinner in the microwave and run out the front door, *for real*.

Do you remember *An Officer and a Gentleman*? Richard Gere throws Debra Winger over his shoulder and takes her out of that miserable factory. Don't we all want someone to carry us away from our jobs, especially if he looks like Richard Gere?

What about *Under the Tuscan Sun*? Diane Lane leaves her past behind to find a new life in Tuscany and, of course, a hot Italian lover. Who wouldn't want that? Yes, movies are the greatest escape for women ever invented.

I wondered what would really happen if I cashed in my 401k and took the next plane to Rome, like Julia did in *Eat, Pray, Love*. I hate to say it, but there would have to be some alterations in this daydream. For starters, I wasn't that crazy about Julia's Rome apartment. I am cold natured, and without central heat in October, I would just die—very sad for me, after spending all that money to fly to Rome. Also, I didn't spot a La-Z-Boy recliner in her apartment, which is a necessity after the age of sixty. Julia didn't have a television, either. How could I watch Netflix? In my fantasy, Rome was beginning to have some serious flaws.

There is also the issue of my diet. While I adore Italian food, I can easily gain ten pounds just looking at pizza and gelato. When you are a smidge over five feet tall, this could spell d-i-s-a-s-t-e-r. None of my clothes would fit after the first week of gorging. Do they sell stretch pants on the Via Vento?

Would I be lonely without my Texas peeps? Julia instantly becomes friends with some beautiful Italians, and they are best pals after ten hot minutes. Would I be able to find beautiful Italian friends who adored me? Maybe it was time to consider India.

In India, Julia goes to an ashram and learns how to pray. The ashram has no air-conditioning and no comfortable chairs, and not one soul looks like they are having a lick of fun. Some people in the ashram take a vow of silence, which is horrifying; I couldn't fathom not talking. They all sit on a hard floor for hours and hours. I have arthritis, so sitting on that hard floor is simply out of the question.

Of course, mosquitos and other strange insects buzz around the ashram. I know I would catch something dreadful and be on ten different antibiotics. The antibiotics would do a number on my tummy, and there would be nothing to eat but rice, curry, and hot tea. My stomach hurts just thinking about it. I didn't need to learn how to pray, either. If I wanted to pray, my church suited me just fine because it has cushy seats. No, I was crossing India off my list for good.

It was time to forge ahead to the land of sunshine, blue skies, palm trees...Bali. Who doesn't love the tropics, the beach, balmy weather, a fabulous beach house, and Javier Bardem? Julia's beach house is simply divine, but there is only one snafu. I didn't notice any central air-conditioning in the adorable cottage, only ceiling fans. I will say right up front that I simply must have air-conditioning, or I can't sleep.

Julia's mode of transportation in Bali is a bicycle. The last time I got on a bike was at a family reunion in Destin, and I did a header in a palmetto bush. I wondered, do they have Uber in Bali?

Every time I go on vacation, the thought crosses my mind, what if I get sick? In the film, even my precious Julia gets hurt and sees a Balinese mystical doctor. I happen to be quite finicky about my body parts, so a Balinese mystic is not in my wheelhouse.

Then there is the thing about my favorite subject, love. Julia falls madly in love with Javier in Bali, and it's just too romantic for words. In real life, Elizabeth Gilbert, who wrote *Eat, Pray, Love*, divorced her "Javier." Real life stinks!

After my little excursion to Rome, India, and Bali, I discovered that there is no place quite like home. I am perfectly happy calling up Domino's pizza, cranking up the heat, and putting my feet up as I lay back in my La-Z-Boy recliner. I think I'll watch *The Holiday*. I never thought of trading houses with someone in England...Now that's a whole new fantasy!

19

Magnolia Market or Bust

Is there is anything better than a trip in May with two of your BFFs? If there *is* something better, I certainly don't know what it could be. Mary Jane, Betty, and I decided that Waco, Texas, would be our fun destination for the day. You might be wondering why anyone would pick wacky Waco. Wasn't it the home of the Branch Davidians? Didn't the Banditos and the Cossacks have a shoot-out at the Twin Peaks in Waco? Isn't that town just a pit stop between Dallas and Austin? The above is all true, but the landscape has changed. Waco now has Texas royalty: Chip and Joanna Gaines.

The Gaines's have single-handedly put Waco back on the map as a "must-see" destination. Here is their backstory. Chip and Joanna are the stars of HGTV's *Fixer Upper*. They redo homes and make Waco's rundown shacks look amazing. Chip takes a sledgehammer to walls, and Joanna shiplaps just about everything. Clint, their best friend, builds Joanna whatever she needs. She wiggles her little finger and tables, benches, bookcases, and mantles magically appear.

Why can't I find a friend like that?

Their home is a farmhouse in the middle of nowhere, and it's precious. They are a precious couple with four precious children, and everything they do is *P-R-E-C-I-O-U-S*. Do you hear me?

Mary Jane, Betty, and I were in dire need some *precious* in our lives. With six kids, two husbands, and one ex-husband between us, I would describe our lives as precarious maybe but certainly *not* precious. We were over the moon because we were on our way to buy us a car full of *precious* and be Joanna Gaines, if only for one day.

Mary Jane, Betty, and I planned to leave early because we knew that Magnolia Market would be a zoo on Saturday. We set sail at nine (which is girl speak for seven), and after only two pit stops, we arrived at the outskirts of Waco. We were in high spirits and sang (to the tune of the theme song from *Green Acres*), "Magnolia Market is the place to be. Farm living, it's for me." During our songfest, Mary Jane almost missed our exit. She popped a wheelie like Mario Andretti, and we made our exit on two tires and a prayer.

As we approached the store, people were running towards it as if it were the Second Coming. Mary Jane commanded us to jump out and save her a place in line. We ran (OK, walked faster than usual) to the back of the line. Women, men, and children were like horses at the gate at the Kentucky Derby; if someone had fired a gun, it would have been a stampede. Joanna hired a lot of young Baylor coeds to help with riot control. The guides told us that six to eight thousand people came to the store *every* Saturday. Any day at the Magnolia Market makes Black Friday seem wimpy.

When we finally got to the front of the line, we had our credit cards clutched in our sweaty palms. Betty yelled, "*Charge*," and that's just what we did! We took off in different directions, grabbing candles, wreaths, wall hangings, bookends, T-shirts, and flowers.

After an hour and a half, we all made it to the checkout line. When guess what happened? Mary Jane spied Joanna's mother. (We had seen her once on an episode of *Fixer Upper*.) We jumped out of line in a flash and followed the poor woman around the store.

She was working in the store that day! I'm sure she wondered why we were stalking her. We were secretly hoping Joanna was in the store, and Mama would lead us to the Promise Land...No such luck.

By now we were starving (shopping will do that to a girl every time—it's exhausting!) and searching for food. On the side of Magnolia Market is a gigantic grassy play area for children, and food trucks are everywhere. We ran to the food trucks. After sampling sushi, barbeque, pad thai, and a corn dog, we felt a little yucky. We passed around some Tums, and we each had a Coke with lots of crushed ice in it. Tums and a Coke cure just about everything under the sun.

Fire the rockets and launch the missiles! After refueling our engines, we were off and running again at full speed. Our next stop was Harp Design Studios. We were almost there when Mary Jane's phone rang. Mary Jane's husband was calling to see if we were on the way home yet. We died laughing over that one.

Harp Design Studios is Clint's store. (He's the guy who makes all the furniture for Joanna.) We were just so sure we would have a "Clint sighting," but Clint was in hiding. Joanna's mother must have called ahead and said three stalkers might be coming his way. We bought a few things and headed for our next stop: McGregor, Texas.

We saddled up, rode hard and headed straight for McGregor. Our fascination with McGregor was the Magnolia House, the B&B that Chip and Joanna built. The little overachievers expanded their precious empire with furniture, paint, a bakery, and now they were remodeling a restaurant in Waco, Magnolia Table. My BFFs and I agreed that Chip and Joanna were beginning to give us all a serious inferiority complex.

Mary Jane's phone rang again. Yes, it was her husband. *Sigh.* He wanted to know how close we were to being home. Without a moment's hesitation, she told him we were gassing up in Waco, but the traffic was *horrible*. Mary Jane told the best fibs ever! Betty and I felt a twinge of guilt about Mary Jane's fibs but not enough to curtail our adventure.

We knew about the Magnolia House because we saw the episode where Chip and Joanna spent Christmas Eve there with their families. Everyone looked so happy on the show, and the house just *screamed* Christmas. The Magnolia House was a perfect little whitewashed home with a well-manicured yard. We circled the house but couldn't get close because it has a gate around it. Betty spied a man walking around, and she waved to him.

"Helllloooo, can you tell us about this *precious* B&B?"

The poor man came over. He just happened to be the caretaker. We fired questions at him like he was on *60 Minutes*. He said that the last guest had just checked out, and the next guest would arrive in about an hour. Betty was just about to ask him if we could *please* come in and look around before the next guest arrived. (Betty has always had a way with men, the little vamp.) Before he could answer, an interloper joined our group! She had the gall to start asking questions of her own. How dare she? Now all hope of us getting inside for a sneak peek was lost. We collectively gave her the *stink eye*, and we got back in the car.

Our last stop was the Cedar Chest Antique Mall where Chip and Joanna shopped. We didn't buy a single thing, but we made a very bold move. We asked the clerk if she could *please* give us directions to Chip and Joanna's home. We explained that we weren't stalkers, but we needed a tiny little peek at that *precious* farmhouse. She shook her head and said that they didn't give out that information to *anyone*. I doubt that Pope Francis's privacy is guarded more than Chip and Joanna's.

Mary Jane proclaimed that the party had to end sometime; it was time to head home, or she would be in the dawg house. All of a sudden, I spied a road sign for Crawford, Texas. My heart started beating fast, and I yelled for Mary Jane to follow that sign. *Now!* I just *had* to see where George and Laura Bush lived and where Jenna got married. But Betty joined forces with Mary Jane (the traitor), and I was overruled. They attempted to cajole me with promises that we would *definitely* go there next year.

On the way home, we made one final stop at Whataburger. We grabbed some burgers and ice tea which delayed us even more. We returned to the car at the precise moment the phone rang—but no one wanted to answer it, especially not Mary Jane.

I mean, really, what can she say?

It was already 5:00 p.m., and we had a two-hour trip back to Dallas ahead of us. Mary Jane's husband was not in a good mood. "Mary Jane, where *are* you?"

For some crazy, inexplicable reason, I decided to "man up" and take the hit for her. I grabbed the phone away and shouted, *"Freedom's just another word for nothin' left to lose!"*

I'm really in the *dawg house* now!

Part Four

Mirror, Mirror, on the Wall...

Mirror, Mirror on the wall...
whos the fairest of them all?

I like myself a whole bunch lately, and I hope you do, too. Maybe self-appreciation is the ultimate gift from old age. Throw in an ex-husband, two kids, four grandkids, and a little bit of hard-earned wisdom and your life suddenly seems pretty grand.

And, by the way, if anyone hasn't told you lately, you look great just the way you are! Embrace those wrinkles and each gray hair because, my friend, you've earned them. You are an original work of art, a masterpiece. You, the bomb, baby...

20

The Lipstick Chronicles

The answer to life's problems, according to my mother, was simple; bright-red lipstick was the solution for *absolutely* everything under the sun. One tube of red lipstick was the magic elixir that could cure tiredness, a bad cold, a bad marriage, a double chin, and bags under your eyes. It was transformative. My mother would remind me daily that *red* lipstick would make my teeth look white, and it would make me *sparkle*.

I purchased my first tube of lipstick at age thirteen from the Dixie Rexall drugstore in Montgomery, Alabama. The importance of this occasion surpassed getting my period, first bra, and high heels. That exquisite tube of lipstick meant that finally, I was all grown up.

All the popular girls in my seventh-grade class thought red lipstick was hideous. Was it conceivable that my mother could be wrong about something? Pink Vanilla lipstick was the color of choice for all the girls at Whitfield Middle School. We all desperately wanted to be a clone of Sandra Dee, Annette Funicello, or a California surfer girl. Since I was the skinny, gawky, nerdy girl with a bad perm, it was Pink Vanilla to the rescue.

After the first week of school, I cautiously tried on Pink Vanilla for my mother one evening. She convinced me that the color was all wrong for my skin type, and worst of all, it made me look washed out. With great fanfare, she dug into her pocketbook and handed me a brand-new tube of fire-engine red lipstick. Now this lipstick was *definitely* my color, she proclaimed.

Yes, I did follow her crazy advice because aren't mothers supposed to always be right?

The next day, when I arrived at school with my bright-red lipstick on, the popular girls stared at me in disbelief. I saw them snickering to one another and pointing at me. My nickname for the next three long, miserable years was "Bloody Lips." Thanks, Ma!

Experience taught me that my mother's sage beauty advice was sorely lacking.

I needed a new look for high school because I wanted to make a grand impression. Millie, my closest confidante, was my best hope. She suggested that the "Cleopatra" look would be the perfect solution for me. Her inspiration came from the blockbuster movie *Cleopatra*. To achieve the Cleo look, she draped my eyes in heavy eyeliner and double strength mascara. She slathered a nude lipstick all over my lips but admitted that something didn't look quite right.

Millie dyed my hair jet black and whacked it into a bob with bangs. My friend never met a challenge that she didn't love! I congratulated Millie on a job well done. We were so proud of the transformation that we planned a grand *reveal* for my parents.

It didn't go quite as planned.

Dad looked up from his newspaper, and he stared directly at me. Finally, he spoke. "You look like someone who's taken up residence in the city morgue." He went back to reading his paper.

Mother exploded. "How many times do I have to tell you? Red! Wear red lipstick!" She was livid. "Do you have any idea how long it will take to grow out that navy-blue hair of yours?"

Six long months, as it turns out, was the correct answer.

At last, I was off to college. My new life was busy with frat parties, football games, and sorority pledging. I found time to upgrade my lipstick to Avon's Fuchsia Flirt. I was so busy that I hardly had time to study, and I was kindly asked not to return to the hallowed halls of academia the following year. I assign much of the blame to Fuchsia Flirt.

For the next twenty-three years, I was busy raising children, a shaggy dog, and a colonel in the army. There was little time for lipstick (which, now that I think about it, might have contributed to my divorce). If I did put lipstick on, it was usually in the car while driving. With the dog in my lap and swatting misbehaving kids in the backseat, I'd put on lipstick—a feat I always managed without peeking in the mirror.

In my forties, I was "suddenly single" and back in the dating game. Every new divorcee needs a fresh look, which for me meant a new lipstick shade. I breezed through several: Candy Kane, Razzle Dazzle, Peach Parfait, Cherries in the Snow, and Bronze Goddess. Ah, those were the good years...and if I say so myself, my lips were dazzling to behold!

Today lipstick is a real dilemma for me. I have cracks and crevices around my lips and must exercise extreme caution when wearing red lipstick. One smudge and I look like my mouth is hemorrhaging. If I wear a pale-pink or nude shade of lipstick, I look like I should be in the ICU and given the last rites. Orangey lipsticks make my teeth look yellow, certainly *not* a good look. What's a girl to do?

I had a drawer full of half-used lipsticks, and I was fed up! I marched into Nordstrom's to the Chanel counter. I threw myself at the mercy of the lipstick consultant and explained all the lipstick dilemmas I've encountered my entire life. Then the seas parted, and all was good in Lipstick Land.

"My dear, the most popular shade of lipstick Chanel has *ever* sold is Rouge Coco 428. We can't keep it on the shelf; every woman needs to own at least *one* thing by Chanel."

Yes, Coco 428 is slightly red…Why, oh why, are mothers always right?

21

Call the Fashion Police...
It's an Emergency!

I blame it all on Jamie Lee Curtis. I really do! But if I'm honest, I must accept partial responsibility. It started with me believing what Jamie Lee had to say was the gospel, and she was Joel Osteen. I am not surprised that I had faith in her because I have this strange malady of trusting celebrities, as I am sure you have gathered by now.

My trust issues began years ago (just ask my therapist) with Jane Fonda. Jane was selling her workout video and assured me that I could look *just* like her if I purchased her video. I bought the video and exercised right along with Jane—but after six grueling weeks, I bore no resemblance to her or anyone related to Jane. OK, maybe I did look a little like *Henry* Fonda, but is that a good thing? Years later, Jane revealed that she had lots of plastic surgery and maybe it did help, just a wee bit, her appearance on the video. I would like to slap Hanoi Jane.

A few years later, Suzanne Sommers sucked me into buying the thigh master. She promised me gorgeous legs if I would only buy her contraption. After using the thigh master religiously for a month, my reward was a pulled groin muscle. I hobbled around in pain, and my legs were still jiggly, wiggly, and dimply and bore no resemblance to Suzanne's. I got sucker punched once again.

After that, I swore off listening to celebs…That is until I watched the *Ellen DeGeneres Show*. Ellen had Jamie Lee Curtis on, and I do love me some Jamie Lee. Jamie Lee braved the cover of a magazine with nary a stitch of makeup on. Ladies, that took some huge cojones! She wasn't airbrushed, and there was no digital retouching. She said that movie stars look just like us except they have makeup artists and cameramen working their magic on them; it's all smoke and mirrors. Inferiority complexes around the world breathed a huge sigh of relief.

Ellen and Jamie expounded on fashion, and I couldn't wait to hear what Jamie Lee had to say. Jamie Lee was sick of trying to put outfits together and trying to figure out what went with what. She didn't have the time or the inclination. Oh, Jamie Lee! You are preaching to the choir! One day, she had an "aha" moment. All her clothing selections from that point on would only be in four colors: black, white, gray, and silver. She showed the audience her closet at home, and it looked perfectly color coordinated. She never had to worry about packing for trips because everything went together, and it was very cost effective. Color, she stated, would only be used for accessories. Ellen nodded in agreement (don't you just *adore* Ellen?), and the audience clapped loudly.

Jamie Lee made me start thinking about all my fashion errors and omissions. My closet was filled to the brim with clothes that were every color of the rainbow, and nothing was color coordinated. I had sweats, faded T-shirts, torn jeans, yoga pants, and a few dresses in plastic sacks. Karl Lagerfeld, the creative director for the house of Chanel and Fendi, once said, "*Sweatpants are a sign of defeat.*" OK, Karl, I'm waving the white flag! I surrender. Call the fashion police and have me cuffed.

Month after month, I painstakingly replaced my wardrobe while my bank account dwindled. The Black and White store became my second home. I banished my favorite red jeans and pink T-shirt to the local thrift store without even a fond *adieu*. Jamie Lee was right; I didn't have to worry about my clothes anymore. What could be wrong with this plan?

Everything!

The black clothes drained all the color from my face and made me look like a vampire in an Ann Rice novel. The gray clothes were just as bad, maybe even worse. The white outfits made me look like a fat Casper the Friendly Ghost. As far as the silver garments go... the only time women really wear silver is New Year's Eve. These colors looked so bad on me that I expected to see an apparition of Joan Rivers appear and give me a tongue lashing.

I must ask myself, "Why did I listen to Jamie?" Was it because Norman Bates killed her mother? (That *still* freaks me out.) Or was it because I had a crush on her dad, Tony Curtis? Of course, Norman Bates had already killed her mom, so I wasn't a homewrecker.

Yesterday, I read something that got my mind off Jamie Lee's advice, once and for all. It was a quote from Kimora Lee (a super-model and designer) that has my head spinning. It's making me go in a completely new fashion direction.

"Always dress like you are going to see your worst enemy."

Now that's something I can wrap my head around...

22

I Hate My Hair!

I had a date with destiny fifteen years ago; I met my greatest pal and confidante, Kevin, my hairdresser. At our first meet and greet, I observed that Kevin was an excellent listener. He let me do all the talking. We would be simpatico.

"Kevin, can you wave your magic hair wand and make me look ten years younger?"

I wanted to say *twenty years younger*, but I didn't want to intimidate him at our first meeting.

Not waiting for his reply, I pressed on and threw out this challenge. There would be special occasions where he would have to be my hair wizard: weddings, funerals, graduations, and the dreaded family photographs. After much thought, Kevin accepted this daunting challenge. (Years later, he confessed that he thought he was being punked.)

Like all men, Kev has good qualities and some bad ones, too. On the positive side, he knows more about hair color than anyone on the planet, and he can cut hair like Edward Scissorhands. He also has a very kind heart. I walked into his salon one day, sobbing that I had been laid off from my job and I might be residing under a bridge shortly. He didn't charge me one red cent for a cut and color that day. What's not to love about a guy like that?

Plenty!

Kevin keeps a running dossier on me, and I don't like it one little bit. This document contains all my "hair" brain ideas over the past fifteen years. My most notable ideas would be trying to look like Julia Roberts, Jennifer Lawrence, and Jennifer Anniston.

The first hair experiment was to look *exactly* like Julia Roberts. As if talking to a child who is a slow learner, Kev patiently explained that Julia doesn't look like Julia. She has extensions, hairpieces, and three beauticians spritzing, spraying, and fluffing her hair around the clock. I looked him straight in the eye, and in no uncertain terms, I told him that I wanted my hair to be long, curly and Julia Robert's red. Kev acquiesced and put the red hair dye and highlights in my hair.

Mystifyingly, I didn't look like Julia. The hair color was exactly the right shade, but something was wrong. The long hair made me look tired, and that particular shade of red cast an orangey glow over my face.

"Kev, Julia's hairdo makes me look exhausted and orangey, so please fix it."

God bless Kevin, he didn't utter, "I told you so."

Six weeks later, my spirits were renewed. I handed Kevin a picture of Jennifer Lawrence.

"Kev, I want my hair short, and I mean extremely short, just like Jennifer's."

He wrote all this down in his dossier (damn him!) and gently explained to me that Jennifer's haircut was difficult to maintain, and short hair was a lot of work. Kevin pointed out that I hadn't quite yet mastered the art of the round brush, curling iron, teasing comb, flat iron, mousse…and maybe this was a little too ambitious for me.

"Kev, don't be silly…Chop, chop away."

Six miserable weeks later, my hair was flat as a pancake. I couldn't do anything with my short mop, and this idiotic hairstyle accentuated my double chins, which was *disastrous*. Jennifer Lawrence and I now had only one thing in common; I looked like a cast member of *The Hunger Games*.

I was back in Kevin's chair once again. Tentatively, he inquired what I had in mind for my hair that day. *Mea culpa, mea culpa*...I'd learned the errors of my ways. All pictures of Jennifer Lawrence were banished forever. He wrote down all my comments about Jennifer and my short hair fiasco like a mad scientist.

Sheepishly, I pulled out a picture of Jennifer Anniston.

"Kev, I have been thinking...I want to grow my hair out long and layered just like Jennifer. I think blond highlights could be super sexy and fun."

Kevin looked exasperated. He explained that I didn't have the coloring to be a blond. He waxed on about how blond hair would make me look washed out. He stated emphatically that I was a brunette, once and for all, and I needed to stay in that lane.

"No, Kevin, I want blond, and I mean *platinum*-blond, highlights."

He scribbled away, and then mixed up the blond hair dye.

Weeks later, my short hair was finally growing out. I hated my limp, straggly blond hair with my dark roots sprouting out everywhere. Jennifer Anniston wasn't that great either. After all, Brad did dump her for Angelina. I felt defeated! Then I spied a *People* magazine with Natalie Wood on the cover. She was smiling directly at me as though giving me a secret message from the tomb.

"Kev, it's plain and simple. I want to look *exactly* like Natalie Wood."

I shoved her picture right in his face, grinning from ear to ear.

"Yes, that's certainly a change for you. I see now that you want a long, dark bob." Kevin furiously wrote all this down, while adding, "You know you are going to have to let your hair grow out, and it's going to be challenging."

"Hush, cover up the highlights please. I don't know what I was thinking going blond."

And he didn't say a peep...

When I walk in for my hair appointments today, Kevin hands me his stupid dossier before I can even sit down. When I bring in pictures of Jennifer Lopez, Christina Applegate, and Sarah Jessica Parker, he refuses to even look at them. Instead, he recites verbatim all of our previous experiments in terror. Begrudgingly, we both decided that I am, once and for all, a brunette with short hair and some red highlights. (I won on the highlights.)

I must confess...Kevin is the longest relationship I've ever had and probably the best one, too! I love you, man...

23

The Case of the Mysterious Talking Feet

In my early years, my feet were happy feet. They didn't complain, whine, moan, or gripe about a darn thing. Life was excellent, and they played nicely in the sandbox with the rest of my body. In retrospect, it would appear that my feet indulged my youth. From cheap shoes to go-go boots, they never uttered a word of complaint.

When I became a working girl, my feet found their voice. My job had a stringent dress code; close-toed high heels were a daily requirement. High heels in every color of the rainbow filled my closet to the brim. On a tight budget, I was always squeezing my feet into shoes that were too small, too tight, and often the wrong size, but they were always on sale. When I returned home from work each evening, my shoes were the very first things I took off and left by the front door. I could faintly hear my feet give a small sigh of relief. This oddity was attributed to my overactive imagination.

One sunny morning, my podiatrist gave me some awful news. Foot surgery was now on my agenda due to prolonged and excessive foot abuse. Oh, pain is something I avoid, and hospitals make me break out in hives! What to do? Pain is *not* my friend.

My feet uttered their first sentence as the anesthesia was wearing off.

"This is *your entire* fault. Just look at us now. We look like a freak show."

For two weeks, crutches and ice packets became my constant companions. Those toes of mine grew even more vocal. "Ouch, we're throbbing and stinging. It hurts and there is too much pressure. For pity sakes, go lay down."

My feet begged me to have plastic surgery for my ugly, deformed little toe, but their sob story fell on deaf ears.

As the years passed, my feet became very opinionated! While shoe shopping, they would offer unsolicited advice. When a pair of leather high heels was in my hand, the noise erupted.

"Drop them now!" my toes commanded.

Hating to be told what to do, I tried them on anyway. All ten toes joined the fray. "Ouch, take the shoes off right now, *girl*, because you are killing us." Not wanting to cause an unpleasant scene, I ran to the comfortable shoe section. You know the place where no woman under fifty would be caught dead.

Things continued like this well into my sixties, but now things have gotten unmanageable. I was invited to a fiftieth wedding anniversary party, and a stunning outfit with matching shoes was a *must*. If my calculations were correct, I wouldn't have to stand more than two hours, so high heels might work this one time. Experience had taught me that after two hours of standing, I would tackle an NFL linebacker for the first available chair.

On this auspicious shoe shopping expedition, my feet were scolded and told to keep a code of silence. I didn't need their opinions, either! In Nordstrom's, I spied some sexy high heels that would be perfect for the party. The heels had only been in my hand for a hot minute when…

"Girl, you have *got* to be kidding. Put those shoes down and get real."

I hurriedly walked toward the sale rack, not wanting to cause a scene. Some strappy silver sandals caught my attention. The shoes slipped right on my foot just like I was Cinderella. My moment of bliss was rudely interrupted.

"That damn shoe is pinching us, and the strap is too tight," my feet wailed.

In defeat, the comfortable shoe section became my only viable solution. I tried on a pair of black shoes that looked like something a nun would wear, but oh my, they were so comfortable.

"Oh yeah, baby," my toes shouted in unison.

You know the stupid black shoes came home with me. Don't dis me...It's ten against one!

Part Five

Men-on-Pause

*S*uddenly single in my forties, I thought my life would be exactly like Carrie Bradshaw's (from Sex and the City). I began a mad search for Mr. Big and looked for madcap girlfriends like Samantha, Charlotte, and Miranda, who were Carrie's BFFs.

But the real world is nothing like a television show. In my world, all my girlfriends had to work hard for a living. Our shoes were from the sale rack at Dillard's, and no Manolo Blahniks were in our future. We didn't go out every night to trendy bars, and alas, no Mr. Big chauffeured us around in limos. The only Mr. Big I found weighed 280 pounds and lived at home with his mother!

You'd think I would have given up the ghost of Carrie years ago but not so much...

24

Never Say "I Love You"
on the First Date

Can you imagine being abruptly thrown into the dating world at the age of forty-five? The word *terrifying* describes it pretty accurately. The world I left behind twenty-six years ago was in a galaxy far, far away. My old life had law and order, dating rules and regulations. Boys asked girls out for a specific date and time with an agenda for the evening. They knocked on your door, met your parents, and promised to have you home before midnight. Young men dressed nicely, and belts held their pants up without a butt crack in sight. Men didn't talk like drunken sailors on a liberty pass—at least, not around girls. That was the world I left behind in 1966.

Fast-forward thirty years; I reentered the dating world as a middle-aged divorcee. The language, customs, and attire had changed, and the new dating rules were puzzling, to say the least. My first immersion into this brave new world began with a man I shall always fondly remember as "Rick the Prick."

After taking a two-year sabbatical from men, I finally agreed to go on a blind date. Rick was a customer of one of my friends, and she assured me that he was perfect for me. With a great deal of trepidation, I walked into the local watering hole, and there stood Rick. I ran through my checklist. He was cute (check), taller than me (check, check), and wasn't drooling (check, check, check). The cute, non-drooler walked up to me with a swagger. There was a hint of haughtiness in him that I immediately didn't like (uncheck). Rick couldn't wait to tell me that he was a high-priced lawyer with one of the best law firms in Dallas (uncheck, uncheck). The gunslinger never asked me one thing about myself (uncheck, uncheck, uncheck).

After the waitress took our order, Rick was excited to tell me that he had created something to save us both time and money.

OMG, is this moron going to try to talk me into a pyramid scheme?

Rick began spouting off about his new credo, "Rick's Rules." The first rule concerned his "critical drive time." If he had to drive out of his zip code for a date, he stated, he was spending the night, no questions asked. I was a problem; I fell into the "zip code–challenged" category.

Before I could grab my smelling salts, Moses grabbed his tablet and read the second commandment. If I were lucky enough to go out with him again, rule two would apply. Rule two stated that all expenses on future dates must be split down the middle. Rick the Prick started pontificating on the third rule when I cut him off at the pass.

"Rick, before you launch into the third rule, I want to share with you my one and only rule: I never associate with fools."

That was the last time I saw Rick.

I had learned my first lesson in the new world: Some men think women over forty should be grateful to be asked out. In their minds, they are doing you a tremendous favor.

Here is my response to that: save the favor, boys and pass the ammo.

A few months later, my friends pleaded with me to give the dating world another try and the lecture series began.

"You are entirely too picky!" my so-called friends said. "You should go out with a man at least *three* times before you decide."

Heeding their advice, I met an older man named David at my gym. This hunk of burning love was a retired navy pilot and we seemed simpatico. After a few weeks, he asked me out for happy hour.

Um, he was taking our relationship nice and slow which I liked. This might lead to the romance of the year (check).

I met him at a local watering hole. David gave me a warm hug and we sat down. The hug was the right touch, warm and inviting. We chatted amicably for the first fifteen minutes, and it dawned on me that I liked this guy (check, check, check). David leaned in close and said there was something he wanted to tell me.

Oh my, is he going to say how beautiful I am or how he wants to spend more time with me? My cheeks flushed just thinking about what he might say.

"I'm living with my ex-girlfriend for financial reasons only, you understand. We haven't had sex in *months*, and I'll be moving out very soon. So please *only* call me at my office because I don't want to make things worse at home."

(Uncheck, uncheck, and uncheck.)

David was mopping up Merlot from his face when I exited stage right.

Ladies, here is lesson number two: Never ride in the backseat, honey. If you can't ride shotgun, stay home.

After Rick and Dave, I was so disgusted with men and their bad behavior that I resigned myself to being single *forever*. No more dating for me! No more disappointments! Who needs men?

Then...the Rainmaker appeared.

Yes, my drought was over! The Rainmaker danced around me and worked his magic. We met at work. Our relationship bloomed slowly and without the hassle of dating. He was handsome, young, intelligent…and best of all, he "got" me. The Rainmaker made me laugh, and for me, that was the greatest hook of all. He was covered from head to toe in *checks*.

The moment came when the Rainmaker and I had our first official date. I was so giddy I began speaking in tongues. I said the three words that no sane woman should ever say first.

"I love you."

The Rainmaker popped his umbrella and ran for cover.

My friends were aghast at my outrageous behavior. They couldn't believe that I had committed the cardinal sin of dating. Numerous suggestions about how I might correct this egregious error were nonstop. After much deliberation and three bottles of merlot, the consensus was that I could tell him one of three things: I was commode-hugging drunk, I was heavily medicated, or I had an identical twin pranking him. That night I put my hand on the girlfriend's bible and swore on wine corks that I would never say those three heinous words again.

But the Rainmaker surprised me and asked me out again. On the second date, I gave a memorable repeat performance. When a girl is dying of thirst and finds a watering hole, anything can and will happen.

25

Blind Dates and Other Calamities

There is a reason some social encounters with the opposite sex are called blind dates. You have to be blind, deaf and dumb to go out on one. I already know what you are going to tell me… my friend Sue met her husband on a blind date, and they are giddy with joy and blah, blah, blah. Anyone who's been single for any length of time will tell you an entirely different story. Take me, for example.

My last (and I do mean last) blind date was as epic as Jack clinging to Rose while the *Titanic* went down. Curt, my next door neighbor, was the culprit. Cupid arranged for me to have a date with one of his friends, a retired airline pilot. Being the eternal optimist, I began thinking of all the benefits of dating someone who had airlines passes. I visualized us having croissants on the Champs-Élysées, dining at La Pergola in Rome, or being serenaded by a gondolier in Venice…

As Bruce Willis would say, dreams die hard.

The mystery man called the next night, and I was filled with anticipation. We chatted amicably until he asked me what I looked like. Wasn't this oaf interested in my sparkling personality, my dazzling charm, and my rapier wit? He delighted in telling me that all his friends thought he was a dead ringer for George Clooney. If he looked like George, would he need a blind date? He would pick me up at 5:00 p.m.

Oh, I forgot to tell you that his name was Dick, which says it all, doesn't it?

No one wants to go out in the middle of the afternoon and eat dinner at five o'clock unless they reside in a nursing home. Everyone knows that women over forty must have soft lightning to mask their very slight imperfections, not glaring sunlight. In case my premonitions about Dick were all wrong, I needed to look my best if I wanted to be George Clooney's new wife.

The doorbell rang and the mystery man had arrived. I opened the door with a big smile on my face and hope in my heart. My smile vanished quickly. Dick stood there, looking more like Pee-wee Herman than George Clooney. He was quite a bit shorter than me, and I am barely five foot four in heels. He wore a fashion faux pas, white shoes. White shoes are only acceptable for a man if he works in a hospital, serves ice cream out of a truck, or has a tennis racket in his hand.

Dick was in a hurry for us to get going. Perhaps I was wrong about him. Could he have something fabulous up his sleeve to surprise and delight me? Did I mention that I reside in the land of delusion?

When we got in his sweet ride, he asked *me* where we should go for dinner. Uh-oh...he had broken the cardinal rule of dating. He didn't have a plan! Gosh, I didn't have a clue what adults did at 5:00 p.m. on a date. Begrudgingly, I suggested a moderately priced Mexican restaurant close to my home, in case I needed to pull the parachute. My suggesting a cheap restaurant made Dick smile from ear to ear.

In the car trying to break the ice, Mr. Excitement shared a few things about himself. He was a real homebody who loved watching television and going to bed early. I bantered back that I was a night owl who loved going out. Dick snarled.

At the restaurant, we headed directly for the bar, which I realized later was the only good thing about the evening. Dick droned on and on about his favorite subject—himself. He never asked me *one* thing about my adorable self. For all Dick knew, I could be an undercover DEA operative scouting out drug lords.

Gulping down a skinny margarita helped numb my pain and put me in a better mood. We had almost drawn a truce when he spilled salsa all over my new outfit. Mr. Cheapskate never offered to pay for dry cleaning my dress. I wanted to give him a kill shot to the head.

Maybe I am a DEA operative.

Dick excused himself and headed to the restroom where I hoped he would permanently reside. I ordered another margarita as a preventive measure against losing my last marble.

When it was time to pay the bar tab, apoplexy set in. Dick moaned and groaned at having to spend twenty-seven dollars for three drinks. With encouragement from my new friend Jose Cuervo, I fired back. "Oh Dick, I completely understand why everyone says you are *just* like George Clooney."

Dick grumbled, "Well, I think I should just take *you* home now."

Agreed, sir!

When we pulled into my driveway, I jumped out of the car like my pants were on fire and sprinted for my front door. Dick yelled, "Aren't you even going to kiss me good night?"

I am too polite to tell you what I told Dick he could kiss…

26

Danielle Steel...Liar, Liar, Pants on Fire

I am a complete sucker for love and romance. Danielle Steel's romance novels are scattered all over my house. Her stories are pretty much the same: distressed damsel meets hunk of burning love at a dude ranch, on a ship, at the beach, or in a snowstorm. They walk off into the sunset happily ever after.

Being a true believer, I went to a dude ranch, sailed across the sea, lounged on the beach, and yet, love was nowhere to be found. All my hopes were dashed until hope reared its beautiful head when I got a text from Linda. She wanted me to be her date for our fortieth high school reunion.

With three divorces between us and broken relationships scattered everywhere, we were ripe for love. We talked until the wee hours of the morning about the possibility of finding our old teenage flames at this reunion. Thoughts of *Glee* and *High School Musical* danced through our heads as we planned our trip. We agreed this was going to be a blast from the past, and true love was only four weeks away. Here was our itinerary:

Friday, June 3: 6:00 to 8:00 p.m. Beach Boy's Cocktail Mixer (Marriott Lakeside)

Saturday, June 4: 11:30 a.m. to 2:00 p.m. Family Picnic (Oak Park)

Saturday, June 4: 6:30 to midnight Last Chance Prom with the Alex City Band (Marriott Lakeside)

In preparation for this grand occasion, I bought the perfect LBD (little black dress) with high heels to match. Spray tan, gel nails, hair extensions, and teeth whitening were just a part of our ultimate makeovers. (The other items are too personal to divulge.)

The money invested in this venture could have paid for a trip to Vegas at the Four Seasons with a gigolo and his brother thrown in for good measure. But what price love? Maybe Mr. Wonderful was just a plane ride away.

I boarded my flight and squeezed into my seat. As I closed my eyes, my mind drifted back in time. My first teenage crush was on a poor, unsuspecting boy named Terry. I was *crazy* about him and chased him until he surrendered. Alas, I was too much girl for him, even then. Linda's true love was Gary, a cute surfer type. We chased those two like they were America's Most Wanted. I wondered about Terry. What would look he like today? Was he single, divorced, or married? What path had his career taken? Was he a Wall Street trader or a starving artist? I couldn't wait to find out. Maybe the universe would reward me with a Danielle Steel kind of love, at last.

Linda and I hugged it out at the airport and grabbed an Uber to the Marriott. We barely had time to shower, dress and work on our game plan for the evening. We decided to play it fast and loose at the party in order to find love. In case anyone monopolized our time too much, we created a secret code: one tug of the right ear meant *"Help! Get me out of here!"*

We walked into the Dixie ballroom. There sat an elderly woman with name tags on a table.

"I'm sorry," said Linda, glancing at all the old geezers milling about. "We are obviously lost. We are looking for our high school reunion."

"You're in the right place, honey," the name tag lady barked. "What's your last name?"

"No, no, you don't understand," I said very condescendingly. "We are at a *different* high school reunion. These people can't be *our* people. They're entirely too old."

The name tag lady put on her glasses and looked us up and down.

"Aren't you Linda?" she said to my friend. "We shared home-room together. I'm Betsy Parker!" The insane name tag lady rose and gave Linda a bear hug.

Linda looked frozen in time.

Pulling myself together I asked, "Are Terry and Gary on the at-tendee list, Betsy?"

Betsy fumbled through her notes on the table. "Gary will be here tomorrow...and we got the nicest letter from Terry's husband saying that they couldn't make it this year."

"You said Terry's *husband,* Betsy. You meant his wife, right?"

"Oh, I thought *everyone* knew Terry was gay," Betsy replied knowingly.

Linda yanked my arm and pulled me as far away from Betsy as possible. We headed straight for the tiki bar.

"We will have two shots of tequila," I said. "Each."

After that shocking reveal, I wanted to rip Danielle Steel's face off. Where was the man of my dreams? Most of the men at this re-union had beer guts, gray hair, or no hair at all. They were huddled together like fourth graders in a corner of the ballroom. Linda and I decided to divide and conquer. Linda went right, and I headed left. She walked over to a group of men, and within fifteen minutes, they were hanging on *every* word Linda said.

I was so impressed with her vamp skills that I was dumbfounded when she started tugging on her ear frantically. This was my secret signal! I hurried in for the rescue. It seemed that when the men discovered Linda was a nurse (we blame this *all* on name tag lady), they went into a feeding frenzy. The men pelted her with personal stories of surgeries gone wrong, undiagnosed ailments, mystery pains, and some even showed her their battle scars. Linda couldn't take it anymore, hence the ear tugging. We grabbed the next elevator and went back to our room to lick our reunion wounds.

The next day, we decided not to go to the picnic and opted for some quality pool time. We grabbed some Starbucks and off we went. Linda and I swam, read trashy novels, and drank cocktails with little umbrellas in them. Some of our former classmates showed up later in the afternoon, even Allison our homecoming queen. Allison gave us the once-over and moved to the other side of the pool.

"Screw you, Allison," Linda yelled.

She was still in a heinous mood from the previous night. I had to admit that Allison *did* look good and said so to Linda. She put her vast medical knowledge to use.

"Our queen has had Botox, fillers, a boob job, and at least one tummy tuck. Drop fifty *k* on yourself, Debbie, and you would be amazed."

The girl has a point.

By six thirty, we were ready to rock and roll and burn the house D-O-W-N. I had on my sassy little black dress, and Linda was the lady in red. We sashayed into the ballroom, feeling all that and more. Our stated mission was to capture Gary and let cupid connect these star-crossed lovers. I took the left side of the room, and she took the right. After a few minutes, there was a tap on my shoulder.

"Hey, aren't you Debbie?"

"Yes, I'm sorry. I don't recognize you."

"Remember me? I'm Gary and we had homeroom together. Have you seen Linda tonight? Betsy Parker said she was looking for me."

"Of course, I remember you and you look amazing. Linda is right over there. She is the gorgeous lady in red."

I led him across the room.

"Linda, look who I found! Gary's been looking for you," I said victoriously.

Linda jerked around, and her mouth fell wide open. Instantly, she radiated a glow all over her body. Sparks were shooting out of her head like it was the Fourth of July. As the lovebirds chatted, I thought, *This is like watching* The Bachelor, *and Linda had been given the rose!*

Then everything went to shiitake in a handbag.

"Linda, I want you to meet my beautiful wife, Allison. You remember Ally, don't you? She was our homecoming queen…"

All that glitter and glow evaporated from Linda's face instantly. In seconds, the veins in her head began pulsating, and her eyes narrowed into demonic slits. Was this my Linda? Or Satan's spawn?

"Oh, how could we *ever* forget your moment of glory, Allison?" Linda said, ever so sweetly. "But I must say, I always thought it was simply tragic that you had to pay kids to vote for you. And Gary, poor darling, you must owe your soul to Ally's plastic surgeon."

"Oh, I'm sorry," I stammered, checking my watch. "It's time for Linda's medication but it was so nice seeing both of you."

We stood outside and I commanded her to breathe. Linda's mascara was running down her face, and hives were popping out on her neck like popcorn. I slapped ice on her face, and gave her a Xanax, and she downed a tumbler of chardonnay.

I gave her my best Vince Lombardi speech.

"Girlfriend, I don't give a rat's ass what anyone thinks about us. We are going back in that party, and we are kicking butt and taking names."

I grabbed our high heels and threw them in the dumpster. "Let's dance…"

We headed straight for the poor, unsuspecting DJ.

"Play Gloria Estefan's 'Conga' if you know what's good for you, buddy."

We started a conga line and a few people joined in the fun. We launched into the Chicken Dance followed by the Cotton-Eye Joe, and we were on a roll. At midnight, the only people left were us, the cleaning crew, and the DJ. I slipped the DJ a twenty to play one last song, which would be our anthem for the evening, Gloria Gaynor's "I Will Survive."

I've got all my life to live,
I've got all my love to give…
I will survive…

The two disco dollies headed to the elevator, proclaiming that we would survive as long as we had each other…

27

King of the Throne

Have you ever spent time on a search and rescue mission, looking for a missing husband? Look no farther; he is hiding in the bathroom.

A man considers the bathroom his domain, an alabaster throne room, which he rules from his porcelain seat. Several times a day, the king must visit this room as he has the arduous task and laborious duties that must be contemplated and resolved, regardless of time constraints. With his earplugs attached to his smartphone, he absorbs all the pertinent information of the day. For a brief respite, he amuses himself with reading, fantasizing, solving crossword puzzles, and contemplating his navel. The king considers his time well spent because he must be educated and well versed on current affairs, so when his wisdom is sought by his loyal subjects, the answer is perfect. After ninety minutes, the monarch exits his throne room without a shower or even a shave.

And if the perplexed queen is audacious enough to ask what he did with all his time in there, his response, brought down to her level of understanding, is, "That's where I do all my thinking, my dear."

A queen, on the other hand, spends no more than five minutes in the bathroom "powdering her nose," so to speak. She waits until the very last minute before doing her duty on the throne. Unlike the king, she can't wait to leave. And as soon as she sits on the throne, chaos erupts in the castle, demanding her immediate attention. It's her young children on the other side of the locked door.

"He took my phone, and you need to come out *right* now and make him give it back," the princess squeals while whacking the prince with something heavy and hard, most likely a book.

The king joins in the festivities and begins banging on the door because he doesn't appreciate anyone keeping him from the place where he does his *business*.

"Where are my glasses? Have you seen my car keys? Don't you *understand* that I am going to be late for work? You need to come out right now!"

And sadly, this is the beginning of the queen's bladder issues.

The king's second place of business is where his royal coach is parked, the garage. The garage offers the king many things—solitude, respite, and social engagements. The royal family avoids the garage because they are smart enough to realize that it is a big, hot mess, a man cave unleashed. The queen will never enter the garage unless it's an emergency and she needs Christmas decorations.

Sometimes, the king becomes lonely and forlorn; he needs the Knights of the Round Table for companionship. The king signals his male subjects, surrounding his realm, to come hither. If the door is wide open to his man cave, the knights may enter, but if the door is closed, the king is not receiving guests.

The garage festivities begin when the knights arrive dressed in their appointed armor—flip flops, shorts, T-shirts, and their custom-fit helmets: baseball hats turned backward.

As the men gather, side by side, they stand in a straight line staring out at the horizon, never looking directly at one another. No words are spoken because the favored form of communications is back slapping and grunts.

The court jester cranks ESPN up to full volume and hands each knight a red chalice, also known as a solo cup, filled with the king of beers, Budweiser. They enjoy a rowdy game of darts and drink until the vat is almost empty.

But at sunset, when the merriment has come to an end, an ominous black cloud lingers over the castle. The world weighs heavily on the king's shoulders; it's the financial affairs of his kingdom.

He fears the queen is spending all his gold coins!

He roars at the queen, "Why did you buy that? You already have a black dress. We don't need any more Christmas decorations! OMG, you bought another pair of shoes? How many shoes does one queen need?"

But the queen's all-time favorite roar from His Royal Majesty is: "Do you really need a cleaning lady? I can start helping out around here."

The queen gives a knowing smile. Should she mention the Bowflex machine, the Yeti cooler, and the Harley Davidson motorcycle all collecting dust in the dungeon? No, the queen keeps her silence because she is wise beyond her years. She gives the king a slight nod and then does exactly what she damn well pleases. Long live the queen!

Part Six

"Mutha's in the Hood" a.k.a. Motherhood

You see an ad in the newspaper. "Wanted: a Mother. Responsibilities include, but are not limited to, cooking, cleaning, doing laundry, grocery shopping, party planning, ironing, and performing carpool duty. You must be an excellent teacher and have superb nursing skills. You will be required to work seven days a week and be on call twenty-four hours a day. We offer no PTO benefits or company holidays. There is no salary or overtime pay offered at this time. Unfortunately, there is not a 401k or any type of retirement plan. The length of your employment, should you accept this position, will be until you drop dead from exhaustion.

"There are some physical requirements for this position as well. For a nine-month period, you will be required to gain thirty pounds. Your body will be stretched and pulled beyond recognition. After the nine-month period, you will push a baby the size of a small watermelon out of your body. You might be required to do this several times.

"We accept all women; we do not discriminate based upon religion, ethnicity, age, or political affiliation. We are flooded with applications daily from around the world, so please be patient. Good luck!"

28

Mutha's in the Hood

You're in the prime of life and the world looks dazzlingly bright! You can have Ben and Jerry's, a pizza, two beers, and you don't gain a single ounce. You dance until dawn, change clothes, and return to work without ever skipping a beat. One starry night, your world turns upside down. The prince, at last, has arrived.

As Johnny Cash says, "We *got married in a fever, hotter than a pepper sprout.*"

Married life is awesome-sauce. You and Prince Charming are always going to football games, movies and dinner. It's a constant party with fringe benefits. A few months later, the doctor has a little "fun" surprise for both of you. Soon yours will be a party of three.

For nine months, your waistline expands along with your hips, and ugly stretch marks spread all over your stomach. Your boobs grow exponentially, and all your new underwear looks like something your grandmother wore. You reassure yourself that soon everything will be back to normal and you can hit the "fun button" once again. After all, how much trouble can one tiny baby be?

A few months later, you're pushing a small watermelon out of your body. It's the hardest thing you have ever done. The nurse brings a tiny bundle of blue and puts him in your arms. Life will never be the same. His name is *Angel.*

The first week home with the new baby goes very well. Mom is there to help with the cooking and cleaning. Hubby has taken the week off, too, and he is helping with the midnight feedings. You pat yourself on the back, "You got this!"

The second week home, everything goes to hell in a handbasket because everyone has vanished. The baby's staring right at you like you're supposed to know what to do. You haven't showered in four days, and sleep deprivation is the new normal. If hubby looks at you the wrong way, you burst into tears. It finally dawns on you that it is sink or swim time. You choose swimming.

Welcome to the terrible twos. Unfortunately, Angel's favorite word is *no*. Each day Angel is crying, falling, peeing, pooping, yelling, and spitting food in your face. He is cutting a tooth, getting diaper rash, or coming down with a cold. Full-blown temper tantrums are a daily occurrence. These are called the" glory days" for a reason.

Angel enters kindergarten. You wave to him as he walks into school for the first time. He looks so little, and a big lump is in your throat all that day. The checkbook is a daily reminder that it's time to go back to work. Your job no longer seems "cool." It's just a necessity of life. Feeling guilty is the new norm because neither job nor child is getting your full attention.

In second grade, Angel is struggling in school. You have a conference with his teacher, and you are dismayed when the teacher doesn't quite understand that your child is brilliant. Angel's gifted, you tell her, and why does she have him in a group with slow readers? You decide, then and there, that you are going to make sure next year Angel gets a "good" teacher.

Life rolls merrily along as you arrange play dates for Angel and attend all his school functions. He plays organized sports for the first time: tag football and baseball. You are sure he is ready for the Major Leagues. So far, this is your favorite age because he is so sweet and tells you everything about his day.

Your boy finally graduates from elementary school, and now it should be smooth sailing. Angel is excited and ready for middle school, or is he? You stay up nights, thinking about drugs, school shootings, and bullying. Somehow, despite all these evils, he survives…and thrives!

In the throes of the eighth grade, Angel confesses that he has a crush on a girl at school. He is going to ask her to the school sock hop! The next day, his eyes are filled with tears because she said, "No thanks." You'd like to tell that little witch a thing or two, but hubby puts a gag order on you.

One day you notice that Angel spends a tremendous amount of time in the shower and he keeps his bedroom door locked. His voice changes, his face breaks out, and you see stubble on his chin. *OMG*, this is the beginning of puberty! You aren't ready for a *teenager*. You take a deep breath and direct hubby to have the "talk" with Angel.

It's time for Angel to get his learner's permit. He masters how to drive with one hand on the steering wheel while the radio blast lyrics that sound like a foreign language. Your car insurance rates soar, and should anyone in the family have a fender bender, you'll all be riding the bus.

Angel is never *ever* alone. He drifts in and out of the house with his posse. He closes his door a lot (which you definitely don't like), he plays music so loud it rattles the roof, and family dinners become a thing of the past. Lately, Angel won't tell you *anything*. When you do get him to open up, he just grunts, "I'm *fine*, Mom." Then he begs you to please let him have a tat, drive a motorcycle, and stay out past curfew. When your answer to his numerous request is *no*, the two of you have a horrible fight, and he tells you that he can't wait to move out. He screams that you are the worst parent *ever!* At least he doesn't accuse you of being a serial killer. You've become the bad cop. Your sweet Angel has vanished into thin air.

But you don't give up, not ever...

Angel's senior year is a blur...homecoming, football games, the yearbook committee, prom, and college applications. One day, Angel comes bursting through the door. "I've been accepted to the University of Tennessee!" he shouts with glee. You are stunned. That university is miles and miles away from you.

Is your baby boy really leaving?

All of a sudden, Angel looks like a young man! *How did that happen?* As he walks across the stage at his high school commencement, your heart skips a beat. He's a graduate! You couldn't be any prouder of him if you tried. Photos are taken, and a celebratory lunch is planned. Angel pleads with you to let him off the hook because he *needs* to go to a graduation party at Jason's house. It's a pool party and the whole senior class is going to be there. You can't compete with that one!

At home, feelings of disappointment and depression pour over you. *My precious boy is all grown up!* While changing clothes, you see a card on your pillow.

Dear Mom,
I want you to know that you are, and always will be, my best girl. I know I have been somewhat of a jerk this year or maybe a complete moron. I am truly sorry. The thought of leaving you and Dad scares me, but it's something I have to do. I guess I have been "breaking away" from you all year long so it will be easier for me to leave. I plan on making you proud of me someday. All my life you have been my role model, showing me what character, integrity, respect, and hard work

look like. If I can grow up to be half the person you are, I will be a big success in life.
You will always be my first real love,
Angel
P.S. Mom, I desperately need a car to take to college.

You can't stop smiling because having Angel was the best decision you ever made.

29

Zombieland

The anticipation of summer can make a mother giddy with joy. Summertime is all about reading trashy novels, taking a beach vacation while having drinks with little umbrellas in them. Each day is crossed off the calendar until you reach the summit, June 1st. This auspicious day is when you officially get your life back. No more driving kids to school while you are in still in your pajamas. Midnight runs to Target for folders, sharpies, protractors, and poster boards cease and desist. Parent-teacher conferences (which you have always dreaded because your kids aren't exactly Albert Einstein) will not happen in your brave new world. The possibilities are endless, and they are right around the corner.

On the first official day of summer, you stretch, yawn, and roll out of bed at seven. The kids are all still sleeping. The house is quiet and peaceful. You pour yourself a cup of coffee and watch the birds in the yard. You go for a long walk, do a load of laundry, make up your bed, and you can't believe how blissful life feels.

At the crack of noon, the first zombie appears. He staggers into the kitchen.

"There's nothing to eat around here, *Mom*. It would be awesome if you would run to Krispy Kreme and get us a baker's dozen."

You decide this is going to be the most spectacular summer ever, and you are going to be the "cool" mom for once. When you return home, bearing the prized doughnuts, the other two zombies are up and staggering around the house with their eyes glazed over and their hands outstretched. The television is booming, PlayStation is roaring, and all three phones are ringing with different ringtones. When the clock strikes two, the zombies are on the move and headed to the pool. Peace is temporarily restored.

That evening, hubby strolls in at six and you tell him to fire up the grill; it's the good ole summertime. You have a cookbook on the counter to inspire him to new culinary heights, Bobby Flay's *Boy Meets Grill*. He sheepishly tells you that there is no propane, but he promises to get some tomorrow. The zombies are beginning their hungry growl. After all, sitting by the pool can be exhausting. You fly around the kitchen and feed the masses.

After dinner, you discover the teenagers in your home are multiplying at a rapid rate. The zombies have invited all their BFF zombies over, and the noise level is literally shaking the windows. You and hubby go to bed at ten, watch the news, and fall sound asleep…at least for a while.

At midnight, the peace is shattered. The zombies are having a karaoke contest. You scream at them and their BFF zombies that the party is *over*. You advise the zombies, "Wake us up again, and it will not, do you hear me, will *not* be pretty!"

Hickory Dickory Dock…it's the beginning of day two of summer vacation.

It's a repeat of the first day and hubby still hasn't bought the propane. You are the chief cook and bottle washer, and the kitchen feels like a towering inferno. The zombies and their friends are squatters. They are doughnut-gulping night crawlers who roll out of bed at high noon with sweaty palms extended, demanding your ATM card. They screech like howler monkeys when you say *no*. They are unemployed, uninspired zombies...and they are getting on your last nerve.

Summer vacation continues and thoughts of being the "cool" mom no longer exist. Law and order must be restored. Your zombies are given one week to find a job or a sport that will occupy vast amounts of their time. After the proclamation, the zombies keep a low profile—huddling in their caves. They hope you won't notice them and the nasty ultimatum will be forgotten.

Mothers never forget a single thing.

It's three days into summer, and hubby still hasn't found time to get the much-needed propane. With a poster board and a sharpie, you print one word on it and place it in the driveway...*P-R-O-P-A-N-E.* Two canisters of propane magically appear the next day.

A few days later, you convene a mandatory war council, and all zombies are in attendance. Each zombie is required to report on their employment status/sports activity. The female zombie speaks first.

"I've joined the swim team at the Y."

Praise the Lord, the plan is working! The oldest male zombie is next.

He grunts, "I got a job flipping burgers."

You and hubby give him a hardy round of applause and tell him that he will never look at a hamburger quite the same way again.

The youngest male zombie reports last. "I'm a manny for the lady next door." He elaborates on his new career choice, explaining that he is now a full-fledged babysitter. You slap your hand over hubby's mouth before he can say that this is a *terrible* idea.

OK, your master plan has come to fruition. Halleluiah!

That night, the house is eerily quiet. The zombies are huddled and contemplating their fate.

The next morning, you hear all this commotion at 5:00 a.m. *What the bloody hell is going on?* The female zombie is banging around the kitchen.

"Mom, hurry up and get dressed. Swim practice is at five thirty!"

Surely, you haven't heard her correctly. Tentatively, you inquire, "Is this just for *today* that you have to be there at five thirty?"

She shakes her head and confirms that practice is at five thirty every morning *five days a week*. You kick your own butt hard because this is a horrible idea. Swim team practice is *definitely* not in your wheelhouse.

The oldest zombie is up by eight. He needs to be dropped off at the burger joint by nine and picked up no later than three. Why hadn't you told the kids that they had to find summer jobs within walking distance of the house?

The last zombie rolls into the kitchen at eight thirty because his manny gig starts at nine. Fortunately, he only has to walk next door. You've always said that he is the smartest one of the litter.

At last! Serenity is once again resorted...until the phone rings off the hook. The youngest zombie is freaking out. The hysteria is related to his lack of babysitting skills.

"Mom, how do you stop a baby from crying? And he keeps spitting his food out! What do I do? Mom, the baby won't go to sleep either."

You are the babysitting hotline all the live long day.

After a few weeks of employment and sports, the kids no longer look like zombies, and the dull glaze in their eyes has disappeared. They are actually going to bed at a reasonable hour. This transformation, however, has nearly killed you. Being the round-the-clock chauffer, cook, cleaner, and 9-1-1 babysitting hotline has been exhausting. You feel like you are starring in *Zombie Apocalypse*. You can't imagine why you were ever looking forward to summer.

One day you drive by their school and look longingly at the front door. You roll down the window and yell, "Open sesame." Just to hear her voice, you call the school principal.

"Hey, Mrs. Wilson, how is your summer going? I wanted to call and make sure that you are OK and that school *does* start on August 20, right? By any chance, do you need volunteers to come in the week before school starts and help the teachers clean the rooms and organize the library? I have three zombies, uh, I mean teenagers who can start today."

"Well, thanks for your generous offer. This is so strange; you are the fourth mother to call me this week, volunteering their kids to help us prepare for the new school year."

You realize you're not the only mother in Zombieland. There are others, lurking out there.

"My three kids will be at the school at eight a.m. sharp, Mrs. Wilson," you say with boundless enthusiasm. "I won't take no for an answer, and I'll pick them up at five."

You feel a twinge of guilty for the first five seconds, and then it passes…

30

A Mother's Best Friend...
the Guilt Trip

Women enter motherhood blindly. They have babies with no earthly idea of what's in store for them. There is no manual or book that teaches poor, befuddled new mothers how to raise good kids. Helicopter moms, tiger moms, and traditional mothers are all trying to figure it out. It's a jungle out there.

We all have different ideas on how to raise good kids. Parents today are polar opposites from my generation. Modern mothers allow children to sleep with them until they are almost shaving. The trusty pacifier has been replaced by Xboxes and iPads. Old-fashioned spankings are now socially unacceptable; the "naughty" chair is the new form of discipline. Thirty-year-olds live at home with their parents until their folks escape to Florida. No judgments here...A mother's got to do what a mother's got to do; wine will take you only so far.

Historically, the guilt trip has been attributed to Jewish mothers and grandmothers, but it's readily available to all mothers. It is an ancient art form that must be studied with great due diligence. Once the skill is acquired, it must be used with discretion. I know because I'm a guilt tripper with the accuracy of a Navy SEAL sniper.

The birth order of your children is essential to long-term success with guilt tripping. Each child will require a different technique and approach. Let's assume you are an overachiever and have four kids. (If you have more than four, a good therapist is the only solution.)

The first child is a born pleaser. He has no peeps or wingmen to run interference for him, so it's two against one, and he behaves. At age three, he is reluctant to pick up his toys, and you counter with how sad and unhappy his behavior is making you. His lip quivers and he puts all the toys away. You can work this kid like a fine-tuned fiddle because he wants *you* to be happy. This technique works well into adulthood if you don't overplay your hand.

The second child should have this motto carved on his chest: *been there, done that.* He has observed his older brother's errors and omissions. The guilt techniques that worked so well with the first child will no longer work with him. When this child is asked to pick up his toys, he responds with a stare. He won't pick up his toys unless faced with bodily injury. You are so frustrated that you use this child as your therapist. You launch into a full-blown rant, listing every injustice perpetrated against you since the age of three. The toys are finally put away because the second child can't take any more drama from his mama.

The third son is by far the most dangerous; he's a born comic. He watched both his brothers have limited success with you, and he's devised a new strategy—making you laugh. You scold him for not picking up his toys, and he makes a goofy face, which makes you giggle. You help him with the toys. He deflects everything with humor; as an adult, he made dropping out of law school seem hilarious. When you finally stop laughing, he will listen to you and do what is required.

The fourth child is a girl and the smartest one in the litter. When it's time to pick up her toys, she starts crying. Dad comes flying in for the "save." She can throw a reverse pass better than anyone in the NFL. She not only ignores your guilt trips, she lobs them back at you with lightning speed. That girl can work it all day long, but you can work it better.

After years of trial and error with my children, I've mastered the art of a group guilt trip, as I am too tired to do it on a case-by-case basis. Recently, I arranged for all my children to join me on a conference call. I alluded that I might be making changes to my will; I had everyone's rapt attention.

"Hello, this is CSI Grapevine, and we have a female corpse here. She had her cell phone clutched in her hand when she passed. It looks like she was trying to text, 'Will someone please call their mother?'"

My phone has been ringing off the hook for days now.

31

Please Stop Crying, Ralph Lauren

A son can try your patience, get on your last nerve, and even give Mother Teresa cause to pause. When he reaches the age of seventeen, it's a time of agony and ecstasy. The agony part is that he will push the boundaries *hard* and argue like Johnny Cochran defending O. J. Your boy will plead with you for no curfews and will look stunned that you won't let his girlfriend "study" in his bedroom. He might insist that you, Scrooge, should fork over money for a spring break fling to Cancun. After all, he will argue, everyone deserves a vacation from the rigors of high school.

In his feeble mind, graduation night is like the Oscars, the CMAs, and the Inaugural Ball rolled into one stellar event. *His* graduation night must include, but not be limited to, a tux, a stretch limo, a five-star dinner, and a corsage for his flavor of the month. He drops to one knee and begs you to be fair for *one time* in your sad little life. His graduation night will cost more than your wedding.

Every day you put your helmet on because you are in a real-life combat zone. No one in the family realizes that you have a severe case of teenage PTSD. *Hang in there!* You have to hold the line until September when he leaves for college, the army, or even the circus. You dream of turning his room into your office.

Some things are etched in your mind forever. I'll never forget my boy's last summer at home. He slept till noon, ate everything not nailed down, and played so many video games that he developed carpal tunnel syndrome in his wrist.

One evening, a month before he left for college, he got the brilliant idea that he needed a new look. His friend's mother, a former beautician, had obviously been dropping acid when she bleached his beautiful black hair a ghastly shade of yellow and cut it into a Mohawk. I tried every conceivable means of punishment to secure the name of this woman who called herself a mother. He and his cronies wouldn't budge one inch with the information. (Maybe they should have considered the CIA as a real job opportunity.) Once his hair started growing back, I calculated that we had barely enough time to buzz his head and hope that only a few yellow strands would be visible to the naked eye. I hoped that his college professors would assume he was turning prematurely gray.

Three weeks before he left for college, we allotted him five hundred dollars for new clothes (circa 1989). I made a list of everything we needed to buy: T-shirts, jeans, one pair of dress pants, and one dress shirt. This was doable if we were careful.

The first argument occurred before we got out of the car at the mall. My son wanted to shop by himself, and he insisted that he didn't need or want his mother's help. He would begrudgingly show us what he wanted to purchase, and then he would be kind enough to let us pay for everything. We were on a collision course going ninety miles an hour. I felt it in my bones. Hubby snapped at me, arguing that I needed to let him grow up and make his own decisions. I threw my list in his hands and stomped into the store. I would deal with hubby later for his decision to defect to the dark side.

After forty-five minutes of wandering around the men's department in Dillard's, our son magically appeared. He declared he needed more money...*much* more money. Our male fashionista had found something he loved—and would fall on his sword for—a pair of white linen Ralph Lauren pants. They cost $145, plus tax. Hubby turned very pale and yelled over his shoulder that he needed to find a restroom. *Coward!*

I screamed at our son to put the pants back. He was acting like he had taken leave of his senses. When I could breathe again, I slowly explained that the pants wouldn't work for a variety of reasons. First, he was going to college in Tennessee where no one wears white linen after Labor Day. Also, linen pants also have to be dry-cleaned, and that requires money that he wouldn't have. He jutted his jaw, and the veins in his head started pulsating. The fashionista declared quite firmly that he was *getting* those pants. I was fed up with him and his father, still cowering in the men's room.

"I am going home now, and I do have the car keys. Anyone who wants a ride home better be in the car in the next five minutes."

Both offenders came running out of the store with the infamous white linen pants poking out of a Dillard's bag...

Four months later, I flew to Knoxville to pay my son a visit and inspect his new living conditions. He lived in a dorm with two other guys. I, of course, did the motherly thing and took everyone out for lunch. I had missed that goofy kid something awful. After lunch, I volunteered to do his laundry. All his clothes were a strange shade of gray and bore no resemblance to the new wardrobe that we had sent him off to school with. As I was tossing his clothes into the dryer, I spotted a foreign object. It was gray and dingy, and the material was funky. It bore a striking resemblance to cutoff shorts. Upon closer inspection, I saw a worn label, barely legible. It said *Ralph Lauren.* I laughed so hard tears rolled down my face.

My boy never waves the white flag! He will tell you today that he loves those dang shorts and wouldn't trade them for anything. Just please don't ever tell Ralph Lauren.

Part Seven

The Last Word

One of the worst flaws about me (and there are so many) is that I must have the last word on any given subject. Please, please don't send me an avalanche of comments because I can just hear you now.

"Oh no, the worst thing about you is your lousy temper and your stellar driving skills."

Please don't remind me that I hate to admit when I'm wrong and you find my infamous "right" dance obnoxious. OK, I get it. I am a very flawed individual. Today is no exception because I simply must have the last word on a few things that have been percolating somewhere in my gray matter.

32

White Food Matters!

The ACLU is refusing to return my phone calls today. I am the new watchdog for all white carbohydrates. My carbs are being blatantly discriminated against by the OEHNs (organic eating health nuts). These people will not stop until they have wiped white carbs off the face of the earth. The OEHNs have even gone so far as to hire an opposition research firm, Fat Fusion, to write a false dossier on my carbs. If you are thinking I'm prone to exaggeration, let me give you a case in point. On restaurant menus across America, cauliflower is the "new" potato, and zucchini ribbons have usurped pasta. I want to protest loudly, carry a sign, and find the closest safe room for a Twinkie and a good cry. Here is my manifesto.

Pillows of creamy mashed potatoes swimming in white gravy can send me into an altered universe. The thought of potato salad with Hellman's mayonnaise makes my mouth water, and my feet do the happy dance. Mr. Spuds and I are madly in love, and it's his versatility that intrigues me. You can bake, boil, fry, and mash the heck out of him without a word of complaint. A word of warning though: you must submerge Mr. Spuds in water because when he gets in a bad mood, like lovers sometimes do, he turns brown. Never throw out Mr. Spuds when he becomes old and tired; he will eventually sprout green shoots. I like to call them plants.

Millions of tourists visit Italy each year on a quest for one thing: pasta. That's how popular my honey is! Pasta drowning in extra virgin olive oil with shards of Parmigiano Reggiano is a culinary masterpiece. Pasta's like the girl next door; she just needs to be gussied up a little bit. Swirl a skirt of pesto around her or dip her into an Alfredo sauce and she is the most popular girl at the party.

Pasta has a practical side as well. It's inexpensive, takes up very little shelf space, and can sit happily in your pantry for a year or more and never go bad. Have you ever seen anyone turn up their nose at mac and cheese?

Just the thought of white corn can sustain me through the dreariest days of winter because it screams *summertime*. You can abuse corn and never hear a word of complaint; shuck it, slap it on the grill, fry it, slather it with gobs of butter and corn won't call the domestic abuse hotline. Corn has the flexibility of a gymnast. It can hop into a salad, dive into a dip, jump into a salsa, skip into a bowl of soup, and land with both feet in a pudding.

Vanilla ice cream is the queen of confectionary delights. It's like an expensive black dress that can be dressed up or down as the occasion requires. You can drown her in hot fudge or let her swim in a sea of caramel sauce. You won't hear a word of complaint from anyone. Drizzle Kahlua or limoncello over her, and suddenly she's a sophisticated lady. The same can never be said for rocky road or butter pecan. They are stuck in their lanes forever.

I can't fight the OEHNs all by myself. I need your help. Fill those grocery carts with corn, potatoes, pasta, and Blue Bell's vanilla ice cream. Let's show them whose boss...

33

Election Night

Peace, Love, Hope

After our recent presidential election, some of my favorite friends invited me out for a celebratory birthday dinner. We were having a grand time until the subject of the presidential election came up. They were on the wrong side of the fence! When asked for my opinion (which is equivalent to opening a can of whoop ass), I told them *exactly* what I thought of their candidate and defended mine like my life depended on it.

As the hours passed, dinner began to feel more like an audition for *60 Minutes* than a celebratory event. After three hours, no one changed their opinion by one iota. Everyone was upset on the ride home, and things haven't been quite the same since. When will I ever learn to keep my big, fat mouth shut? I've thought about that evening more than I should have and realized that something good did come out of it. I had a moment of enlightenment.

We are all in this crazy life together, citizens of this country we call the good ole USA. Presidents come and go; Democrats and Republicans will never see things quite the same way, yet America remains the greatest country the world has ever seen. As much as the news media would like to divide us, I choose to think we are all pretty much the same.

We love our children, and we want them to have a better life than we did. Our pooches and kitty cats are bona fide family members; we can't imagine life without them. Diets never work, and bathing suit shopping is the worst experience ever! We are *never* happy with our hair, bodies, clothes, or makeup. Someone will always act like an ass at family reunions and on New Year's Eve. Our hankies are out in full force at weddings; it's too romantic for words. We can bad-mouth our mother, but don't you *dare* say a word about her. We love the good guys, and we couldn't care less what race, religion, or sexual preference they are, just as long as they are good "peeps."

Milk chocolate, hugs, and a good cry soothe our weary souls. Men and women will never understand one another, yet we pursue one another with a vengeance and marry anyway. Divorce is never easy, and a "conscious uncoupling" is hogwash.

We have zero tolerance for cheaters, liars, and people who think they are better than we are. Grandkids are our passion, and spoiling them rotten is our goal. We shove their adorable little pictures in complete stranger's faces because we are sure they have never seen a child as cute as ours. Real-life love stories like William and Kate make us giddy with joy.

We know for sure that money can't buy happiness, and you can't take it with you when you go. The only thing that lives beyond the grave is the love you give and receive. It's the one thing that gives our life real meaning.

Income tax, root canals, mammograms, and Pap smears are our least favorite things. A garage sale, a Hershey bar, Kevin Costner, and a funny movie can get us in a good mood for days on end. Our girlfriends are our "rock," and who could imagine life without them? Words fail us at funerals, and we have no idea how to heal a broken heart. Baseball and football games are our national pastimes, and everyone cheers their favorite team on to victory.

We proudly salute the flag and honor our men and women in the armed forces. We pray nightly for their safe return home. When the national anthem plays, our hearts swell with pride, and we remember the sacrifices made so that freedom can ring.

No matter where you are in life—be it a young mother, single gal, domestic goddess, or an over-the-hill broad like me—you aren't rowing your boat all by yourself. We've all been there, done that, and made it through to the other side. Put a smile on your face and make a choice to be happy every day. Listen to that little voice inside you that says, "*I think I can. I think I can.*" Paint a picture, write that poem, snap that photograph, and learn to play the guitar. Open that cupcake shop you've dreamed about and dance your dance…

Until next time,
Debbie Klein

Acknowledgments

A heartfelt thanks to Rich Mussler for guiding me every single step of the way on this literary adventure. Lynn Saunders, your brilliant advice and encouragement helped me more than you will ever know. A special thanks to Matt Hosey, Cindy Farrell, and all my besties who believed in me.

A special shout out to my Facebook friends who followed my blog and encouraged me to write this book, I hope you like it.

Made in the USA
Middletown, DE
20 March 2018